Success with

Asian

names

Success with
Asian
names

A practical guide
for business and
everyday life

Fiona Swee-Lin Price

NICHOLAS BREALEY
PUBLISHING
OCM 76828799
LONDON · BOSTON

First published in the UK and the US by
Nicholas Brealey Publishing in 2007

3–5 Spafield Street   100 City Hall Plaza, Suite 501
Clerkenwell, London   Boston
EC1R 4QB, UK   MA 02108, USA
Tel: +44 (0)20 7239 0360   Tel: (888) BREALEY
Fax: +44 (0)20 7239 0370   *Fax: (617) 523 3708*
www.nicholasbrealey.com

ISBN-13: 978-1-85788-378-7
ISBN-10: 1-85788-378-0

British Library Cataloguing in Publication Data
A catalogue record for this book is available from the
British Library.

Library of Congress Cataloging-in-Publication Data
Price, Fiona Swee-Lin.
  Success with Asian names : a practical guide for business and everyday
life / Fiona Swee-Lin Price.
    p. cm.
  Includes bibliographical references and index.
  ISBN-13: 978-1-85788-378-7
  ISBN-10: 1-85788-378-0
  1. Names, Personal--Asia. 2. Names, Personal--Asia--Pronunciation. 3.
Forms of address--Asia. I. Title.

  CS2950.P75 2007
  929.4089'95073--dc22

2006038825

First published in Australia by Allen & Unwin in 2007.

Printed in India by Gopsons.

contents

list of diagrams

list of tables

introduction

When I first started helping people manage cultural diversity, the importance of names never occurred to me. Like most cross-cultural trainers, I assumed that training should focus on 'broader' issues, like communication, racism and cultural values. When I actually went out and talked to people about how I could help them with cultural diversity, however, the subject of Asian names kept coming up.

I was working at a university at the time, so I interviewed staff about their experiences with international students. I spoke to people in a wide range of roles—academics, librarians, maintenance staff, IT support staff, people working at food outlets and information desks—and difficulty with Asian names was mentioned again and again. As my interviewees pointed out, using someone's name is one of the first things staff have to do when making contact with a student, and it is stressful and embarrassing when you are confronted with unfamiliar names which you don't know how to use.

Three key difficulties were commonly mentioned in the interviews. One issue raised by almost everyone was how to pronounce Asian names correctly. A second difficulty was knowing how to address someone with an Asian name. The third difficulty commonly mentioned by administrators was how to enter Asian names in databases designed for Anglo-Saxon names. Based on this feedback, I began formulating what became a half-day workshop called 'Working with Asian Names'. My aim was to provide information and practical advice on how to manage the challenges of dealing with unfamiliar Asian naming customs.

'Working with Asian Names' has been very popular, not only with university staff but with staff from libraries, government bodies, hospitals and other multicultural organisations. However, there's only so much that can be covered in a half-day workshop. So rather than expand the workshop any further, I decided to write the book you are now reading. I hope you find it a useful guide to the diverse and fascinating names of Asia.

about the book

Success with Asian Names: A practical guide for business and everyday life provides a detailed overview of the names of Asia.

Part one provides background information on Asian names, contrasting the languages and Asian cultures from which they are derived with the language and cultures of English-speaking countries. It looks at cultural differences in the way people view names, and explains the different writing systems and name structures used in Asia.

Part two gives the reader detailed information on names from 14 specific Asian languages. Each chapter begins with general background on naming customs in a specific language, providing examples of typical names, information about how names from that culture might be Westernised, and practical advice on pronunciation, how to address people and entering names into databases designed for Anglo-Saxon names.

Part Three helps the reader to identify the country of origin of a particular name and clarifies which languages are spoken in specific Asian countries.

which Asian countries are covered?

The word 'Asian' has different connotations in different parts of the world. In the United Kingdom, the most common use is to refer to the Indian subcontinent. In North America, however, the word 'Asian' typically brings to mind people from countries in North Asia, notably China, Japan and Korea. Australians use a similar definition to North Americans, but might expand their concept of Asia to include South-East Asian countries, such as Indonesia, Singapore and Malaysia.

In this book, 'Asian' refers to Asia in the broadest sense, as a continent which is home to more than 50 countries and hundreds of different languages. This book covers 14 major Asian languages in depth, selected for their number of speakers and the size of their diaspora. Notable Asian languages that have not been covered in this book include *Lao*, the official language of Laos; *Hmong*, a language spoken in the Indo-Chinese hills; *Tagalog*, the official language of the Philippines, as well as other major Indian languages, such as *Gujerati* and *Telugu*. These languages may be covered in subsequent editions.

use of the term 'English speaker'

When I refer to 'English-speaking countries' in this book, I am referring to Western countries where the majority of people speak English as a first language and for whom the most familiar name structure is the Anglo-Saxon system with given name, middle name and surname, in that order. Countries which fall in this category include Australia, Canada, Ireland, New Zealand, the United Kingdom and the United States. Of course, this is not to say that this book is aimed only at people from these countries: it is for anyone who reads English and is interested in learning more about Asian names.

part one

introduction to part one

Names are very important in English-speaking countries. Every time we fill in a form or introduce ourselves to someone, we begin by providing our names, and these are later used to identify us. So long as we have names which fit the boxes on the forms, and are used according to customs everyone understands, this system works well. However, when people from Asian countries with different naming customs visit or immigrate to an English-speaking country, many challenges can arise.

Asian names can be difficult for English speakers. Most difficulties are related to three key issues. The first is the way people use and perceive names, which can differ considerably from culture to culture. This issue is addressed in chapter 1.

The second key issue is language. English speakers often struggle to pronounce Asian names because they are derived from Asian languages and the letters in them are not necessarily pronounced or combined in the way they are in English. For example, the q in 'Qing' is pronounced ch in Mainland Chinese Mandarin names. Asian names may also contain combinations of sounds and letters which do not exist in English. For example, the letters **uy** are commonly found together in Vietnamese names.

The reason behind the confusing spelling of many Asian names has to do with romanisation: the process of converting a name from its original Asian script into the Roman alphabet which is used to write English. Chapter 2 explains the four different types of writing system used in Asia and how these are usually romanised, and part two provides a language-by-language guide to how letters are pronounced in different Asian cultures.

The third key issue is structure. Names in most Asian cultures do not follow the given name + surname structure used in English-speaking countries. For example, in some Asian regions, names do not contain anything like the English surname; in other regions, the 'surname' is placed first, rather than last. This can lead to considerable confusion about how the person should be addressed and how the name should be registered on a computer system. A further difficulty is that many people living in an English-speaking country adapt their Asian names to fit the Anglo-Saxon structure, a process called anglicisation. This is introduced in chapter 3 and explored in depth in part two.

why don't people just *ask*?

The response of many people when they hear of others struggling with Asian names is, 'Why don't people just *ask* how to use their names properly?' I agree that this logical step is worth trying.

It is not, however, foolproof. If you are meeting someone face to face or communicating by email, you can ask them what they would like to be called, but pronouncing and remembering their answer may still be very difficult. If you are contacting people by telephone from a list, you will have to guess which part of the name to use and how to pronounce it, and hope that you are accurate enough for the person who answers the call to figure out who you are looking for.

You may also find that you do not get the response you were expecting if you ask someone how to use their name properly. Often people with Asian names will offer you a Western name to use, or accept your inaccurate attempt at saying their name and seem reluctant to coach you further on pronunciation. These unexpected responses are related to cultural differences in what names represent to people and will be discussed in more depth in the next chapter.

chapter 1
what's in a name?

No book on names would be complete without a reference to Shakespeare's famous line from *Romeo and Juliet*. In this chapter, the line refers to what names represent to people. Looked at individual by individual, names mean something different to every person. Looked at society by society, however, there are some definite broad differences in what names mean.

When I interviewed English-speaking Australians about their experiences with international students, I was struck by how important they considered names to be. Even people who didn't mind others making mistakes with their own names were often concerned that they might offend Asian people by forgetting or misusing their names. Probing deeper into the issue in interviews and workshops, I discovered that this was because they used given names a great deal, and considered names to be central to a person's identity. Using someone's name correctly is therefore an indication of interest and respect for them as a person; using a name wrongly is considered rude and implies disregard.

Interestingly, almost all of my interviewees took it for granted that Asian people also felt this way about names. However, when I interviewed native speakers of the Asian languages covered in this book, a different picture emerged. It became clear that people raised in different Asian countries perceived names in different ways and that none of them viewed names in the same way as my Western, English-speaking interviewees.

names and status

In my interviews, a common theme that emerged across all Asian countries, from Sri Lanka to Korea, was that people who grew up in Asia used names a lot less than people raised in an English-speaking country. The reason for this seemed to be that throughout Asia, more importance is placed on family and relative status than on individual identity.

This broad cultural difference between Asia and English-speaking countries can be seen in the way names are used. In the English-speaking countries, parents typically choose names for their children based on personal taste, and individuals tend to choose for themselves what they wish to be called in each context. Status still shapes the way people address one another but its role tends to be more flexible. For example, when two English speakers of very different status meet for the first time, the person of lower status typically uses a formal form of address (Dr Gray or Sir, for instance), and the person of higher status decides whether to accept this or invite them to use a less formal form of address (Terence, Terry, doc, mate) at some point in the relationship. In general, however, people are using each others' given names more and more, which implies that the two people are equal, or at least that the status differences between them are being disregarded. The use of given names also suggests a more personal relationship. For example, a university lecturer who asked her students to call her 'Jenny' would be implying a more friendly, personal relationship than one who expected to be called 'Professor'.

The use of given names is particularly widespread in Australia and New Zealand, societies renowned for their egalitarian attitudes, but it is also growing in the United States, United Kingdom and Canada. These countries are often described as *individualist* societies, where there is a strong focus on people seeing themselves as independent beings first and a member of a group (such as a family, a company, a team, etc.) second. In individualist societies there is a strong focus on personal choice, taking responsibility for your own actions, self-determination, self-fulfilment, self-expression and so on. It is therefore not surprising that given names are important to people in these societies: after all, people's given names are what identify them as individuals, more so than their family names, which identify them as a member of a family, or their job titles, which identify them as a member of a profession.

Compared with English-speaking societies, Asian societies tend to place much more emphasis on status and family, and this shapes the way people choose and use names. Selecting a name for a child in many Asian cultures often involves consultation with elder members of the family and other authority figures, such as astrologers or Buddhist monks, and the way the name is used is closely tied to status (measured by age, position

7

in family or organisation, profession and various other factors). People whose status is equal to or lower than your own are typically addressed by name, but those of higher status must be addressed formally, often by title alone with no part of the person's name attached. Whereas English-speaking people usually say 'Dr Smith' or 'Uncle Rob', in Asia it is common to address people of higher status by title alone, as in 'Doctor', 'Uncle' or 'Teacher'. A wide range of titles is in use in Asia; in English-speaking countries, the only titles still widely used without a name appended are 'Sir' and 'Madam' in customer service, family titles like 'Mum' and 'Dad', and 'Professor', which is sometimes used in North America.

The degree to which this is the case varies from place to place, and from person to person. People in modern Asian cities are shifting towards more individualist thinking, and people of Asian background who have lived long term in an English-speaking country usually embrace English-speaking attitudes towards names. In very traditional institutions in English-speaking countries, status still plays a major role in shaping how people address each other. Nonetheless, these broad cultural differences do account for many of the observations that English speakers make about Asian names.

common observations

When I was researching my 'Working with Asian Names' workshop in 2001, many of the English speakers I interviewed were surprised by the way Asian people behaved when dealing with names. Some of the most common observations were that Asian people often:

1. seem reluctant to use the English speaker's given name
2. seem reluctant to correct the English speaker's pronunciation
3. adopt a Western name.

reluctance to use the English speaker's given name

This is most common when the English speaker is of higher status than the Asian person. As outlined above, addressing someone of higher status by their given name is considered rude and disrespectful in Asia, which makes it disconcerting for Asians when they arrive in an English-speaking country and find themselves invited to do so. For example, if Dr Jane Brown asks her 19-year-old students to call her 'Jane', which to her conveys that she is friendly and approachable, some students may try using 'Miss', 'Madam' or 'Dr Jane' because they feel uncomfortable addressing someone they regard as senior to themselves by their given name.

There are two ways of handling this issue. One is for English speakers simply to accept being addressed more formally by Asian people. The other is to explain that in this country it is not considered disrespectful to address someone by their given name; it is considered friendly. This should help the Asian person to understand the informality they see in English-speaking countries, although it may take some time before they feel comfortable addressing people in this way.

It is also important to remember that when the English speaker is of lower status, he or she should *always* show respect by addressing the higher-status Asian person formally, unless invited to do otherwise. If you are not certain of how to use the person's title correctly, check the chapter for the relevant Asian language in this book and, if you can, confirm the correct form of address for that person with one of the person's subordinates or someone from their culture. If these options are not available, address them as 'Sir' or 'Madam' and politely ask how they would like to be addressed.

reluctance to correct pronunciation

This is becoming less common, but can happen, especially when the English speaker is of higher status. To the English speaker, who prioritises individual identity over relative status, asking for coaching in how to pronounce someone's name indicates showing respect and making an effort. To many Asian people, finding fault with someone of senior status is far ruder than mispronouncing a subordinate's name! The Asian person may also know from experience that English speakers cannot pronounce the name, and would rather accept an approximation than dwell on the issue.

If you are struggling to pronounce Asian names, by all means ask the people concerned to help. If correct pronunciation is important to them, they will help you get it right. However, if the person is plainly uncomfortable, and they smile and reassure you that your pronunciation is fine or offer you a Western name, it is better to accept the name they provide rather than pressuring them for coaching to make sure you pronounce their 'real' name 'properly'. Remember also that most Asian people you encounter will speak at least two languages, and will therefore understand that it is difficult for anyone to pronounce a name in a foreign language.

adopting a Western name

Adopting a Western name for use in English-speaking contexts is particularly popular among the Chinese, but may also be seen in other parts of eastern and South-East Asia. Many English speakers say they feel embarrassed that Asians feel they have to 'deny their culture' by changing their names, and prefer to use their 'real' names instead. (Note that this is very much the thinking of people who rate individual identity above relative status!) Asians who adopt Western names typically think of this as a practical measure which makes life in the host country easier, not a denigrating practice forced on them by incompetent English speakers.

Remember that Asians who adopt Western names are usually doing so to make it easier to operate in an English-speaking context. If someone offers you a Western name by which to call them, it is absolutely fine to use it: don't feel you should press them to tell you their 'real' name and how to pronounce it. Insisting on using the person's Asian name instead of the name they offer you can come across as presumptuous and pushy rather than 'culturally sensitive', especially when the other person is of equal or higher status.

where do these differences come from?

Why is it that names represent different things in Asia and the English-speaking societies? An interesting theory is that this is related to religion and ideology.

The dominant religion in English-speaking countries is Christianity, and in the last few centuries, the people in power in these countries have been Protestant (except in Ireland). An important feature of the Protestant religion is that it focuses on the individual. Worshippers do not need to go to a priest for confession, as in Catholicism; they pray directly to God Himself, and take upon themselves the personal responsibility of upholding His commandments. The Protestant work ethic, which states that people get what they work for, also reflects the idea that each person should take control of their own future. It seems plausible that the importance placed on names in English-speaking societies ultimately relates to the focus on the individual in Protestantism.

Although there are significant Protestant minorities in some Asian countries (notably Korea), the fundamental values in those societies come from other religions and philosophies. A particularly influential ideology in eastern Asia is Confucianism. Confucius was a Chinese philosopher who is thought to have been born around 551 BCE. He viewed the family as the central unit in society and placed considerable importance on education, and showing respect for one's teachers and elders.

Chinese names and those in other countries where Confucianism has been influential (notably Korea and Vietnam) illustrate this emphasis on family and seniority. Confucian names are written with the family name *first*, implying the importance of the family. This is traditionally followed by a generation name shared by same-sex siblings, with the personal name unique to each individual placed *last* (although occasionally you will see the personal name placed before the generation name).

Hinduism, which originated in India, is a hierarchical

religion. It organises people into castes of ascending status, and centres around a belief in reincarnation, where someone of lower caste who leads a good life can rise to a higher caste in the next life. Surnames in Hindu communities indicate the caste and family to which a person belongs, and given names are often derived from the names of the many Hindu gods and goddesses. Because of the religious significance of Hindu names, Hindus rarely adopt Western names and place importance on correct name use.

Buddhism also has hierarchical elements, though these are less central. The founder of Buddhism was a man called Siddhartha Gautama, who outlined the eightfold path that people should follow in order to achieve freedom from the suffering involved in the cycles of life, death and rebirth. Buddhist parents traditionally consult a monk or astrologer when naming children, to ensure the children are given names which will be auspicious for their time of birth. Other naming customs vary across different Buddhist communities, though it is becoming popular for Buddhists in Indo-China and South-East Asia to give children names in Sanskrit, the language in which Buddha's teachings were written. The importance of detachment from personal desire in Buddhism discourages people from placing too much importance on the correct use of their names.

Islam originated in Arabia and was brought to south Asia and South-East Asia by Muslim traders. Muslims follow the teaching of Muhammad, whom they believe is the last of God's many prophets (many of whom are familiar Biblical figures, such as David, Moses and Jesus). Some Muslim communities in Asia, notably the Malay people, give their children Arabic Muslim names like those found in the Middle East. These names typically have religious significance: they are often derived from characters or passages in the Qur'an, and a lot of Muslim men are given the name Muhammad (often spelt Mohamad in South-East Asia) or one of the many variations on the names of the Prophet. For this reason, Muslims believe that names are important and almost never adopt a Western name, which would be seen as a 'Christian' name. Other Muslim communities, such as the Javanese of Indonesia, favour names from the local language.

There are many other religions and ideologies in Asia, but the above discussion of some of the major ones illustrates how they influence the way people choose, use and perceive names.

summary

People raised in Asian countries typically place more importance on status than do people in English-speaking countries. This means it is important to them to know a person's status and age relative to themselves, and address those of higher status formally and those of equal or lower status informally. Names tend to be used a lot less in Asia, because people of high status are often addressed by title alone. English speakers, who tend to be more egalitarian, may find that Asians are uncomfortable with addressing superiors by their given names, and may be reluctant to correct the pronunciation of people senior to them.

In individualistic English-speaking countries, names are connected with personal identity and it is considered respectful to let people choose the name by which they wish to be addressed and to use it correctly. Because of this, the decision of people from countries in East and South-East Asia to adapt their names for use in Western countries may be interpreted by English speakers as a 'denial of their culture'. For the most part, however, the Asians who Westernise their names do not see it this way because they do not make the same connection between names, identity and respect. The adaptation is simply a practical measure that makes it easier for English speakers to use.

tips on cultural differences

- Keep these cultural differences in mind, but do not necessarily assume they will apply to everyone of Asian appearance. People of Asian origin who were raised in an English-speaking country, or have been living in one for many years, usually adopt Western attitudes towards names.
- If someone offers an English name, they have chosen to do so and it is acceptable and correct to use this name.
- Do not pressure someone to coach you on the pronunciation of their 'real' name if they seem reluctant.
- If someone who sees themselves as younger than and/or junior to you insists on addressing you formally, you have two options: either accept the formal address, or explain that in your country it is considered friendly and polite to address everyone by given name, regardless of status.

chapter 2
understanding Asian languages: romanisation

One of the main reasons why English speakers find Asian names difficult to pronounce is because the letters in many Asian names are not pronounced the way they are usually pronounced in English. In many cases this has to do with how the name has been converted from the original Asian script into the Roman alphabet used in English, a process called *romanisation*.

This chapter will explore the difficulties associated with romanisation, and then explain the five main types of writing systems used in Asian countries and how these are romanised.

about romanisation

When Europeans began writing Asian languages in the Roman alphabet, they used their own languages as the basis for spelling. Languages in regions that were colonised by the British were spelt according to English pronunciation, but languages in other regions were romanised for speakers of other European languages. One of the reasons why English speakers can struggle to pronounce Asian names from some countries is that they have been spelt to suit speakers of Dutch, French or Portuguese.

Another issue is that most Asian languages contain sounds which do not exist in English. The following three methods can be used for romanising such sounds:

1. nominating a roman letter to represent the sound, preferably one pronounced reasonably close to the actual sound
2. inventing a combination of letters to represent the sound
3. adding a *diacritic* to a roman letter to modify its sound (diacritics are marks like the accent on the e in the French word café).

A simple illustration of method 1 is the romanised Japanese word 'karaoke'. The sound represented by an r in karaoke is not the same as an English r, but a sound which falls somewhere between an l, an r and a d, which does not exist in English. In this case, James Hepburn, the man who romanised Japanese, decided to use an r to represent this sound, with the result that English speakers pronounce it as an English r.

Method 2 can be seen in Urdu, where kh is used to represent a consonant that sounds rather like a gutteral h pronounced at the back of the throat. Again, unless the English speaker knows and can pronounce the sound represented by kh, the likely pronunciation will probably sound like an English k.

Method 3 has been widely used in the romanisation of Asian languages. For example, in Vietnamese, placing a circumflex over the letter **a** (i.e. **â**) changes the sound from **ah** to something similar to the **eu** in the French word **feu**. The problem with using diacritics in this way is that readers need to understand what the diacritic means in order to figure out how to pronounce the modified letter. Another problem is that letters with diacritics on them are clumsy to use and difficult to enter into a computer. Most Asians with diacritics in their names leave them off for convenience when writing their names on forms in English-speaking contexts, and as computer use increases across Asia, more and more countries are trying to develop romanisation systems which avoid the use of diacritics.

Given the amount of complications involved in romanising Asian languages, it is not surprising that many English speakers struggle to pronounce Asian names. One of the aims of this book is to clarify how letters are pronounced in romanised Asian names, beginning with an explanation of the different writing systems found in Asia.

logographic writing systems

Chinese, Japanese

In the Roman alphabet, words are made up of symbols that we call letters, placed one after the other. Each symbol typically represents one sound. For example, the word **sky** is composed of three symbols placed one after the other, **s k** and **y**, and these symbols tell us how to pronounce the word as a whole. The way the word **sky** looks and sounds does not bear any direct relationship to what the word means.

In a *logographic* language like Chinese, each symbol is not a letter, which tells the reader the sound of the word, but a 'character' or little picture which tells the reader something about the *meaning* of the word rather than spelling out the *pronunciation* of the word. For example, the familiar symbol 🚭 shows a picture of a cigarette with a circle and line through it. The symbol gives the reader the *meaning*, which is that people are not allowed to smoke, but it does not give any details about how it should be *pronounced*: we simply have to learn that it is pronounced 'No Smoking'. This is roughly how symbols from a logographic writing system work.

The ancient character for the word 'sun' was a dot in a circle ⊙	This was changed over time to a version which was faster to write 日

Diagram 1: How pictures became characters

Originally, the symbols were actually pictures of what they represented. Over time, these pictures have been modified, as shown in Diagram 1. More complex words could be formed by combining simple words together, as shown in Diagram 2.

木	+	木	=	林
tree		tree		forest
日	+	月	=	明
sun		moon		bright

Diagram 2: Combining characters to form a new word or concept

Remember that there is no 'spelling' in Chinese characters. Children in China have to memorise that the character 明 means 'bright' and that it is pronounced **míng**: there are no letters to guide them as to how it is pronounced. Instead of learning two sets of 26 symbols, like English-speaking children, Chinese children have to memorise several thousand characters when they are learning to read.

When Europeans first came into contact with logographic languages, they needed to find some way of writing down words in a form they could read. They did this by listening to the words and coming up with a way of spelling what they heard using the Roman alphabet. For example, the Europeans romanised the character 林 as **lin**, because this is how it sounded to them. Using this process, they eventually developed a standard *romanisation system* representing Chinese sounds using the Roman alphabet.

For some logographic languages, such as Vietnamese, the local people eventually replaced the characters with this romanised writing system. In others, such as Chinese and Japanese, the locals continued using characters, and the romanisation system for the language became a tool used for interacting with Westerners.

syllabaries

Japanese

The Japanese use a combination of two different types of writing system. They write some things using characters borrowed from the Chinese logographic script over the centuries, which they call *kanji*, and others using one of two *syllabaries*, called *hiragana* and *katakana*.

Like an alphabet, a syllabary is made up of a limited number of symbols from which all words in a language can be built. The difference is that in an alphabet, each symbol represents one sound; in a syllabary, each symbol represents one syllable. For example, in English, the syllable **ma** is composed of two separate symbols, the consonant **m** and the vowel **a**. In the Japanese syllabary hiragana, the sound **ma** is represented by a single symbol, ま. A further illustration of how this works is shown in Diagram 3.

みつびし		み	つ	び	し
Mitsubishi	=	mi	tsu	bi	shi
とよた		と	よ	た	
Toyota	=	to	yo	ta	

Diagram 3: Mitsubishi and Toyota written in hiragana

The symbols, or *kana*, used in Japanese syllabaries were developed from simplified versions of more complex characters, or *kanji*. Just as the Roman alphabet has two different ways of writing its 26 letters, in capitals (**ABC**) and lowercase letters (**abc**), Japanese has two different ways of writing the same set of syllables: in the curly hiragana, such as those shown in Diagram 3; and the more pointy katakana, in which Mitsubishi is written ミツビシ and Toyota is written トヨタ. Hiragana are used for local Japanese words, and katakana are used for words imported from other languages.

There are 50 basic kana in Japanese, of which about 45 are still in common use. The sounds of many of these can be modified using diacritical marks. For example, the hiragana symbol ha (は) can be changed to ba by adding two short diagonal lines at the top right corner (ば), and to pa by adding a little circle (ぱ).

Romanising a syllabary is a little easier than romanising a logographic writing system. There is a limited set of syllables, and the sound of each one can be transcribed using two or three letters from the Roman alphabet. For example, か is transcribed as ka. Once every syllable has been romanised, any word in the language can be written in the Roman alphabet.

abugidas

Indian languages, Sinhalese, Thai, Khmer, Lao, Tibetan, Burmese

The writing systems used across most of the Indian subcontinent and Indo-China are referred to as *abugidas* (sometimes called *alphasyllabaries* or *syllabic alphabets*). In an abugida, every symbol represents one syllable, as in a syllabary.

The difference between an abugida and a syllabary is the use of *vowel signs*. These are diacritical marks which alter the sound of the vowel in the syllable. For example, in Devanāgarī, the abugida used for Hindi and some other Northern Indian languages, there are 46 basic symbols. Of these 34 are consonants, but not consonants representing a single sound, like those in the Roman alphabet. Each consonant symbol consists of the consonant sound followed by an 'inherent' or built-in vowel. For example, the symbol क represents the sound

ka, with the built-in vowel **a**. The sound of the symbol can be changed to **ke**, **ki** and other variations by adding a vowel sign to it, as shown in Diagram 4. The vowel signs in Devanāgarī are special simplified versions of vowel symbols called *matra*.

Consonant	Vowel (full form)	Vowel sign (simplified matra form)	New symbol
क + ए ka + e		ऐ simplified to this =	के ke
क + ओ ka + o		ऻ simplified to this =	को ko

Note: dotted circle in column three indicates where basic symbol should be placed.

Diagram 4: How vowel signs change the sound of abugida symbols

Abugidas are typically romanised by giving each vowel a Roman alphabet equivalent (e.g. ए is written as **e**), and each basic consonant is given a consonant plus vowel combination (e.g. क is written as **ka**). For symbols with vowel signs on them, the consonant remains consistent and the vowel is replaced (e.g. के is written as **ke** substituting the original **a** with an **e**).

The difficulty with this process is that languages which use abugidas often include vowel sounds for which no established roman equivalent exists. For example, in Hindi the vowel **a** can be pronounced either as in the English word **ma** or in the same way but with the **a** sound held for longer. The Roman alphabet does not have a standard way to indicate the difference between a vowel and the

23

same vowel pronounced longer, so people romanising languages with this feature had to invent one. Long vowels are commonly indicated by doubling the vowel, **maa**, or putting a *macron* above it, **mā**. Unfortunately, what these indicators mean in terms of pronunciation will often be unclear to uninitiated English speakers. For example, not all readers will know the long line above the a means the vowel should be lengthened. Diacritics are also difficult to enter into a computer.

abjads

Arabic, Urdu, Hebrew, many Middle Eastern languages

The script used to write Urdu, the national language of Pakistan, and Arabic, in which the Qur'an is written, is a type of writing system called an *abjad*. Most known abjads are written from right to left. An abjad is an alphabet that only contains symbols for consonants. Vowels may be indicated by adding diacritical marks to a consonant, as shown in Diagram 5, or left for the reader to interpret from his or her knowledge of the language.

Although rough Roman equivalents can be found for the consonants in the abjad, the absence of clearly fixed vowel sounds in abjads complicates the romanisation process. Regional variations in pronunciation can lead to a range of different romanised versions of the same name or word. For example, the spelling of the name of the holy Prophet of Islam varies considerably across the Islamic countries. In Indonesia and Malaysia, the spelling 'Mohamad' is the most common, but in Pakistan the preferred spelling is 'Muhammad' and elsewhere the spelling 'Mohammed' is common. Similarly, the 'Qur'an' may also be spelt 'Koran' and 'Quran'. This book uses 'Muhammad' and 'Qur'an'. (Refer to part two for the preferred spellings in each Asian language.)

	Consonant	Vowel diacritic	Consonant with vowel
Arabic symbol	ن	́	نَ
Roman equivalent	n	a	na

Diagram 5: How vowel diacritics work in Arabic

languages written in other alphabets

Korean, Mongolian

Some Asian alphabets have an alphabet of their own, in which every symbol represents one sound, as in the Roman alphabet. The Korean alphabet, which is called *hangeul*, is the one that English speakers are most likely to encounter.

An interesting feature of hangeul is that words are not formed by letters placed horizontally from left to right, but are arranged together in a 'box' to form a word, as shown in Diagram 6. The initial consonant, for instance m, is placed in the top left corner, the vowel in the top right corner, and the final consonant, if there is one, is placed on the bottom of the box.

Romanising a language which uses another alphabet involves deciding which Roman letters best represent the sounds of letters in the other alphabet. For example, the letter m is used to represent the Korean letter ㅁ, because the sound of these two letters is the same. When the Roman alphabet has no direct equivalent for the sound in the other language, the foreign letter is represented either by the roman letter or letter combination which comes closest to the original pronunciation. For example, the symbol ㅈ does not have precisely the same sound as an English j, but j is used nonetheless because it is the letter which sounds most like the original Korean sound.

ㅁ		ㅏ		ㄴ		만
m	+	a	+	n	=	man

Diagram 6: How hangeul symbols are combined to form a word

languages written in the Roman alphabet

Vietnamese, Indonesian, Malay, Tagalog

A handful of Asian languages are written in the Roman alphabet. In some cases, such as Vietnamese and Tagalog, this is because the local people have decided to replace the existing writing system with the romanised writing system developed by the Europeans when they came to their country. In other cases, such as Indonesian, this is because the language was originally a spoken language used for trade, for which Europeans developed the established written system.

Note that the way words are spelt in these languages will reflect the language of the Europeans who developed the system! When the romanisation system is developed by the British, as it was with Malay, the way names are pronounced is generally logical for English speakers. When the language is romanised by a speaker of another European language, the result may not be a logical guide to pronunciation for English speakers.

The first romanisation system for Vietnamese was developed by Portuguese missionaries, and this system was edited in the 17th century by a French Jesuit priest called Alexandre de Rhodes. As a result, Vietnamese names are spelt in a way which reflects French and Portuguese pronunciation rather than English pronunciation. Like French, Vietnamese writing incorporates a wide range of diacritical marks which modify the way letters are pronounced. A familiar example of a diacritical mark is the accent on the e in the French word café, which changes the sound of the e to an ay sound. Some of the diacritical marks in Vietnamese change the sound of the letters, as shown in Diagram 7, and others refer to tones, which will be explained in the next section.

Roman letter		Diacritical mark		Modified letter
a (pronounced 'ah')	+	^ (circumflex)	=	â (pronounced like the 'e' in 'pert')
d (pronounced 'dz' in North Vietnam, 'y' in South Vietnam)	+	¯ (macron)	=	đ (pronounced like the 'd' in 'dog')

Diagram 7: Examples of diacritical marks used in Vietnamese

27

As mentioned earlier, there are two main problems for English speakers with the use of diacritical marks in Asian names. The first is that they rarely know what change in sound the diacritical mark is meant to indicate. The second is that even if they learn what the diacritical marks mean, most people with Asian names leave the marks out when writing their names in an English-speaking context, which means there is no way of knowing how to pronounce the letters correctly (e.g. whether the letter is really an **a** or is actually an **â** with the circumflex omitted).

tonal languages

Chinese languages, Thai, Vietnamese, Lao, Mon

English speakers use tone of voice for expression. When someone says 'She's there' as a statement, the pitch goes down at the end of the sentence; when saying 'She's there?' as a question, the pitch goes up at the end. When English speakers reach the end of a list, for example when reading out a phone number like 7939 3322, the voice tends to drop at the end, in this case on the last '2'. English speakers also use pitch to emphasise certain words: compare 'I want to *see* you' (not just talk to you on the phone) with 'I want to see *you*' (not him).

In a number of Asian languages, the way you pitch your voice when saying a word is a fundamental part of its meaning. That is, saying a syllable with the pitch of your voice going up means something different to saying the same syllable with the pitch of your voice going down. The classic illustration of this is the five different

28

Character	妈	麻	马	骂	吗
Romanisation	mā	má	mǎ	mà	ma
Meaning	mother	hemp, numb	horse	to curse	(question mark*)

* Placing this character at the end of a statement turns it into a question. For example, in Mandarin 'How are you?' is 'Ni hao ma'—Ni is 'you', 'hao' is good, hence 'You good?'

Diagram 8: Illustration of tones in Mandarin

meanings of the word **ma** in Mandarin, as shown in Diagram 8.

All of the five characters shown in Diagram 8 are pronounced **ma**. However, the diacritical marks over the **a** determine how the word should be said to indicate which of the five words is intended.

1. the first character is pronounced with a high, level pitch (called 1st tone), represented either by a straight line over the a, **mā** or a number 1, **ma1**.
2. the second character is pronounced with a rising pitch (2nd tone, similar to the way you would say 'What?' in a shocked voice), represented by an acute accent, **má** or a number 2, **ma2**.
3. the third is pronounced with a pitch which goes down and then up again (3rd tone), represented by a caret, **mǎ** or a number 3, **ma3**.
4. the fourth is pronounced with a falling pitch (4th tone, similar to the way you would say a firm 'No'), represented by a grave accent, **mà**, or a number 4, **ma4**.

29

5. the fifth is pronounced in a short, neutral way (no tone), represented by writing the letter without any diacritical mark or number, **ma**.

Any Chinese, Thai, Lao or Vietnamese name you see will have tones built into it. Strictly speaking, you are not pronouncing the name 'correctly' unless you incorporate these. However, English speakers need not worry unduly: people with names in tonal languages cannot expect them to pronounce tones correctly, for two reasons.

First of all, English is not a tonal language, and many English speakers find it hard to differentiate between different tones, let alone reproduce them. Second, even if the English speaker can detect and reproduce tones and interpret tone markings correctly, the romanised version of the name they see will not have the tone marks written in (e.g. **Zhōu Míng** would be typed into an Australian system as just Zhou Ming).

Realistically, the best English speakers can be expected to do is pronounce the name to the best of their ability. If you have a good enough ear to pick and pronounce the tones in an Asian name when you hear it, so much the better. If you can't, don't worry about it too much— almost all of the Asian people you deal with will be bilingual (or trilingual, or more), and are therefore likely to understand the difficulty of pronouncing words in a foreign language.

summary

Romanisation is the main reason why Asian names can be so difficult for English speakers to pronounce. In many cases, the way an Asian name is spelt is not a good reflection of its pronunciation, as the letters in it represent different sounds from those they normally represent in written English.

tips for pronouncing Asian names

Do your best to pronounce names correctly, but bear in mind that in many cases you will not be able to pronounce them exactly as they sound in their native language unless you are a very gifted mimic. This is because the way names are spelt often does not give you enough information to pronounce them perfectly, and in many cases names will have features like tones or sounds which you may find almost impossible to use because they are not present in English.

If you know which Asian language the name is from, consult the appropriate chapter in part two of this book to figure out a good approximation of the pronunciation and write a phonetic version underneath the name if necessary. This can help you if you need to address someone in person or read their name aloud. If you do not know which Asian language the name is from, you may be able to identify this from the guide in part three.

chapter 3
adapting
Asian names:
anglicisation

Anglicisation is the process of adapting a name to make it look more like an Anglo-Saxon name so that it is easier for English speakers to use.

Names from most Asian countries are not structured like Anglo-Saxon names. In many countries in eastern Asian, the family name (similar to the surname) is placed first, and in other parts of Asia people do not have surnames at all. This can make it difficult for English speakers who need to know how to address someone, or how to enter an Asian name into a database.

Asian people frequently try to confront this difficulty by changing their names into something which resembles the Anglo-Saxon given name + surname structure. They often do this by nominating two of their names to serve as given name and surname. For example, a Vietnamese woman called Le Thi Thanh Thuy might decide to use 'Thuy' as her given name and 'Le' as her surname, thus producing the name 'Thuy Le'. Another common practice is nominating part of the name as a surname and then choosing a Western name to place in front of it. For example, a Chinese man called Wu Mingsheng might call himself 'Michael Wu'.

Although anglicisation of this kind aims to help English speakers, in effect it often causes more confusion. In most cases, the changes made to the Asian name are unofficial, with the result that the person is known only by an anglicised name which is not on any official documentation. Another problem is, it is not always clear to an English speaker that what they are presented with is an anglicised version of a name. In some cases, the English speaker has carefully learned that the Vietnamese place their family names first, only to encounter a Vietnamese name like 'Thuy Le', where the family name has been placed on the end in imitation of Anglo-Saxon naming practice.

This chapter looks at three different types of Asian names, and how they are typically adapted to fit Anglo-Saxon naming conventions. At the end of the chapter, some suggestions about how to design forms and databases are provided. For more detail about anglicisation in specific languages, refer to the relevant chapter in part two.

Anglo-Saxon names

Names of Anglo-Saxon origin are structured as shown in Diagram 9. This is the pattern English speakers are most familiar with, and they know exactly how it works. They know that in informal situations people are usually addressed by their first name (or an abbreviated version of it, e.g. 'Chris') and that in formal situations people are usually addressed by title plus surname ('Mr Wilson').

They are familiar with the small set of titles used in English-speaking countries. They also know that children inherit their father's surname, that wives traditionally change their surnames to their husband's surname after marriage, and that it is usually possible to identify a person's gender from the given name.

Title	Given name	Middle name (or 2nd given name)	Surname
Mr	Christopher	John	Wilson

Diagram 9: A typical name of Anglo-Saxon origin

Unless they have learnt otherwise, most English speakers assume that all names fit this pattern. When confronted with an unfamiliar name, they will typically use the first part for informal address and the last part for formal address, preceded by the appropriate title for the person's gender.

For example, it would be natural for an English speaker to see a patrilinear name like Siti Azizah binti Osman and assume that this person should be addressed as 'Siti' in informal contexts and 'Mr Osman' or 'Ms Osman' in formal contexts. Without understanding how Malay names are structured, the English speaker would have no way of knowing that 'Siti' is a name prefix which is not used for address, and that 'binti' means 'daughter of' and indicates that the person is female and her father's name is Osman. In fact, in Malaysia she would be called 'Azizah' informally and 'Miss Azizah' formally, though in English-speaking contexts she might anglicise her name to 'Azizah Osman' for convenience.

Confucian names

The names of people from societies strongly influenced by Confucian thinking (notably China, Korea and Vietnam) follow a distinct pattern. As shown in Diagram 10, they traditionally consist of three one-syllable parts which are called the *family name*, *generation name* and *personal name* respectively.

Family name	Generation name	Personal name	
Leung	Chin	Ho	} brothers
Leung	Chin	Wei	

Diagram 10: Typical Confucian names

The family name is shared by members of the same family, and inherited by children from their father, although women do not usually change their family name to their husband's after marriage. Given the similarity of the 'family name' to the British 'surname', it is an obvious choice when a person with a Confucian name is in an English-speaking context and needs to nominate a 'surname'. You may also see the order family name + personal name + generation name instead, especially among Koreans.

The generation name is a traditional feature which is still common in people from Confucian cultures, although it has been waning in popularity over the past few decades. It is shared by children of the same sex in the same generation. For example, brothers called Leung Chin Ho and Leung Chin Wei share the generation name 'Chin'. Their sisters might be called Leung Hong Mei and

Leung Hong Lian, sharing the generation name 'Hong'. In very traditional families, the boys' generation name may be taken from a family poem written in Chinese characters, with the first character in the poem being used for the generation name of the first generation, the second character being used for the next generation and so on. Occasionally girls and boys may be given the same generation name, a practice which has become more popular in the last couple of decades. (Even families in countries like Vietnam, where the language is no longer usually written in Chinese characters, will still use this traditional naming method.)

The personal name is unique to each individual. Within families, older members tend to address younger ones by personal name alone, and younger members address older members by titles such as 'big sister' or 'father'. In formal situations outside the family, people typically address each other by title + family name (e.g. Mr Leung). In informal situations, the address varies more, but the most usual form is generation name + personal name (e.g. Chin Ho) for Chinese and Korean names, and personal name alone for Vietnamese names.

adapting Confucian names

The first problem confronting a person with a Confucian name in an English-speaking context is the name order. The family-oriented people from Confucian cultures place their family name first; the individualist English speakers place their surname last. As a result, it is very common for people with Confucian names to rearrange their names in English-speaking contexts. They typically do this by placing the family name at the end and calling it a 'surname', and placing the part they use for informal address at the start and calling it a 'given name', as illustrated in Diagram 11. This rearrangement greatly increases the likelihood that English speakers will address them correctly.

Note that Koreans use both their generation name and personal name for informal address (Hyun Jin), like an English 'given name', and they therefore place both of these in front of the 'surname' (Kim) when anglicising their names. By contrast, most Vietnamese people use only their personal name for informal address, and therefore place just this in front of their 'surname' (Duc Nguyen).

English speakers often find Confucian names difficult to pronounce and remember (for reasons detailed in the previous chapter). As a result, many people with Confucian names decide that it is more practical for them to adopt a Western name. This is very common among people of

Original Korean structure	**Family name** Kim	**Generation name** Hyun	**Personal name** Jin
Westernised structure	**Given name** Hyun Jin		**Surname** Kim

Original Vietnamese structure	**Family name** Nguyen	**Middle name** Tran	**Personal name** Duc
Westernised structure	**Given name** Duc		**Surname** Nguyen

Diagram 11: Rearranging Confucian names

Original Chinese structure	**Family name** Wong	**Generation name** Siew	**Personal name** Jin
Western given name, no middle name	**Given name** Sally		**Surname** Wong
Western given name, Chinese names retained as middle name	**Given name** Sally	**Middle name** Siew Fang	**Surname** Wong

Diagram 12: Adopting a Western name

Chinese background, but may also be seen among Koreans and Vietnamese (though less often, possibly because people from smaller countries feel more strongly about their names as a reflection of their national identity).

When people with Confucian names adopt a Western 'given name', they typically use it with their family name alone, as shown by 'Sally Wong' in Diagram 12. The need to put both the Western name they use and the official Asian name on official documents often leads to confusion. Sometimes the generation and personal names are retained and used as a 'middle name', as in 'Sally Siew Fang Wong'. Other combinations may also be seen, such as 'Sally Wong Siew Fang', 'Wong Siew Fang (Sally)' and so on.

patrilinear names

Traditional Islamic names and those from some groups and regions in India and Sri Lanka do not contain any form of surname or family name which is passed down the generations through the father. Instead, the father's given name is passed down to his children, as illustrated in Diagrams 13 and 14.

When people with names like these enter a country with Western naming customs, they usually need to nominate a 'surname'. People with patrilinear names typically nominate their father's given name for this purpose. Jamil bin Abdullah would probably call himself 'Jamil

	Given name	(son / daughter of)	Father's given name
Malay man	Jamil	(bin)	Abdullah
His son	Faisal	(bin)	Jamil
His grand-daughter	Fatimah	(binti)	Faisal

Note: Malays may leave out 'bin' (son of) and 'binti' (daughter of) in English-speaking countries. See Malay chapter for more details.

Diagram 13: How patrilinear names work in Malay

	Father's given name	Given name
Tamil man	Ramanathan	Nandakumar
His son	Nandakumar	Palasubramaniam
His grand-daughter	Palasubramaniam	Renuka

Note: Tamils commonly shorten their father's given name to an initial (e.g. R. Nandakumar). Sometimes other names are also present and shortened to an initial, hence R.K. Narayan. See Tamil chapter for more details.

Diagram 14: How patrilinear names work in Tamil

Abdullah', using his father's given name Abdullah as his surname, and Palasubramaniam Renuka would probably call herself 'Renuka Palasubramaniam', using her father's given name Palasubramaniam as her surname.

unstructured names

The names of people in Burma and some parts of Indonesia do not follow a set pattern. In these regions there is nothing that corresponds to the Anglo-Saxon surname: children's names often share no part in common with their parents' names at all.

	Courtesy title*	Name	Name	Name
Mother	Daw	Kin	Kin	Schwe
Father	U	Paw	Oo	Htun
Son	Maung	Hla	Han	

* Daw is similar to 'Ms', U to 'Mr' and Maung to 'Master'. Note that there is no relationship between the names of parents and child. The Burmese usually include their titles with their names.

Diagram 15: Unstructured Burmese names

	Name	Name	Name
Mother	Yolanda	Pramudita	Sulastri
Father	Hadiman		
Daughter	Ami	Prasang	

Diagram 16: Unstructured Javanese names

When people with unstructured names come to an English-speaking country, they are often confused by the insistence on a distinct 'surname' and 'given name'. What typically happens is that either the last part of the name (e.g. Schwe and Htun in Diagram 15) is used as a 'surname', or the part the person prefers to be addressed by is simply used with a title in formal situations (e.g. Ms Kin Kin Schwe, or Ms Yolanda as in Diagram 16).

A person with only one name, like Hadiman, may do several things. In Indonesia he would be Mr Hadiman in formal situations and just Hadiman (or Hadi) informally. However, many databases in English-speaking countries require people to have at least two names. English-speaking administrators commonly address this problem by putting 'Hadiman' in both the given name and surname fields (making it 'Hadiman Hadiman'). Hadiman himself might prefer to adopt a name of his own choice for use as either a given name or a surname. For example, he might adopt his father's name as a surname ('Hadiman Budiyanto'), or adopt a childhood name or nickname as a given name ('Lantip Hadiman', 'Hadi Hadiman').

summary

Names in many Asian countries are not structured into 'given name/s + surname' like Anglo-Saxon names. Asian people often adapt their names to approximate this Anglo-Saxon structure, and use some part of their name as a 'surname' when the name is used in an English-speaking context. This can cause confusion among English speakers who need to address them or enter their names in databases.

chapter 4 managing Asian names

The differences between Asian names and Anglo-Saxon names can lead to a range of practical administrative difficulties. For example, an organisation with a large number of Asian clients might need to enter their names into a database designed for Anglo-Saxon names. This chapter provides practical tips for overcoming common problems when managing Asian names.

terms of address

With Anglo-Saxon names, English speakers know to use title + surname for formal address and given name for informal address. However, with an unfamiliar Asian name, it can be very difficult to figure out what to call someone. Here are some tips which may help.

- Use formal address—'Sir' or 'Madam'—when you are not sure what to call someone. Being too formal is much better than being too informal, which could come across as disrespectful, especially if the person is of high status.

- If you are meeting someone of high status, they will often be accompanied by staff. Ask one of their staff for the correct way to address the person.

pronunciation

Once you have established what part of a person's name you use to address them, you need to figure out how to say it. If you know the person's country of origin, consult the relevant chapter on that country in part two and use the pronunciation guide to help you. Here are a couple of extra tips.

- It is often easier to remember and pronounce a name if you know how it is spelt. When you hear a difficult name for the first time, get the person to write it down, and try to connect the sound to the spelling.
- If the way a name is spelt does not reflect the way it sounds to you, write down your own phonetic notes. For example, you could write **twee** to help you remember the correct pronunciation of the Vietnamese name **Thuy**.

designing forms

Many of the problems associated with using Asian names and entering them in databases stem from the forms on which these names have been entered. Forms in English-speaking countries typically ask people to enter their title, surname and given name. Sometimes there is also a further space in which to enter 'other given name/s', 'middle name' or 'middle initial'. The spaces into which people are asked to enter these names are frequently divided up into little boxes, into which people are asked to enter their names letter by letter in block capitals. An example of a typical form of this kind is shown below.

Please enter your name in BLOCK CAPITALS:

Title: Mr ☐ Mrs ☐ Miss ☐ Ms ☐ Dr ☐

Surname: ☐☐☐☐☐☐☐☐☐☐☐☐☐☐☐☐☐☐☐☐☐☐☐☐

Given name: ☐☐☐☐☐☐☐☐☐☐   Middle name: ☐☐☐☐☐☐☐☐☐

Diagram 17: Typical design of forms in English-speaking countries

why forms can be confusing

People from countries which do not use a Western name structure are often confused by forms designed for English speakers. Confusion can arise for a number of reasons, including:

- a lack of understanding of what is meant by 'title', 'surname' and 'given name'
- having a name that follows a different structure (e.g. father's given name, given name) which does not fit into the categories provided on the form
- having an unofficial Western name or nickname during their time in an English-speaking context, which they do not know how (or whether) to include
- having a name which has too many letters to fit into the number of boxes provided.

designing better forms

One option for better-designed forms is to provide one long field labelled 'your full name' or 'your name as shown on your passport', and another field where people can enter the name they have chosen to use for English-speaking contexts, as illustrated in Diagram 18. This design accommodates names of any structure, and allows for the difference between the person's official name and what they are actually called.

Title: Mr ☐ Mrs ☐ Miss ☐ Ms ☐ Dr ☐ Other: ☐☐☐☐☐☐☐☐☐☐☐☐

Full name (as shown on your passport):

What you would like people to call you (your nickname, Western name, etc.):

Diagram 18: Alternative form design

If this is not practical, here are some other simple steps that can be taken to help both the people entering their names on the forms and the people who transfer the names into a database afterwards.

- Add an 'other' option under 'title', thus allowing space for people who have titles that are not included in the standard Anglo-Saxon structure.
- Use 'family name' or 'family name/surname' rather than just 'surname'. 'Family name' is the preferred term in many parts of Asia. Most people from countries

where names do not include a surname nominate part of their name to use as a surname soon after arriving in an English-speaking country.

- Allow at least 18 letters for the 'family name/surname' field. Many people from Thailand and south Asia have family names which exceed 15 letters.
- Allow at least 15 letters for the 'given name'.
- Do not use the terms 'first name' and 'last name'. These terms can be confusing because they imply order—remember that people with Confucian names place their surnames first, not last.
- Never use the term 'Christian name'. This may confuse or even offend people who are not Christian.
- Don't include a 'middle initial' field—it is better to have one long field for 'given names'.
- Include a field where people can enter the unofficial name they may be using in an English-speaking context. This could be labelled 'What would you like us to call you?', 'Western name or nickname', or 'preferred name'.

It is also important, when designing forms, to be aware of who will be using them. If you know the forms are to be used by a specific group, you can tailor the forms accordingly, as outlined below.

- If the users are from Thailand, southern India or Sri Lanka, where people have very long names, you can make sure you have as many boxes as you can fit in for the name fields.
- If a significant number have limited English or a low level of education, you can label the name fields as simply as possible (e.g. 'What would you like us to call you?' instead of 'Preferred name').

- If most of the users are from a particular language group, it may be helpful to label the fields in that language, as well as English.

databases

It is common practice for the information on printed forms to be transferred to an electronic database. If the design of your forms matches the design of your database, it should be easy to transfer information from one to the other. If not, it will be necessary to sort the information from the forms into the fields provided by the database.

Having to 'sort' information into database fields may not be a bad thing. For example, the Cantonese Chinese name Kitty Cheung Kit Yee and the Tamil name Janahan Sivakumar are very different in structure, as shown below.

Cantonese Chinese name	Western name	Family name	Generation name	Personal name
	Kitty	Cheung	Kit	Yee
Indian Tamil name	Father's given name		Given name	
	Janahan		Sivakumar	

Diagram 19: Comparing the structure of a Cantonese Chinese name with an Indian Tamil name

These names can, however, be entered into a database in a way that shows the English-speaking reader how to use them correctly. This can be done by placing the part of the name used for informal address under 'preferred name' and the part used with the title for formal address under 'surname'. From Diagram 20, it is clear to an English speaker that Kitty Cheung Kit Yee would be 'Ms Cheung' in formal contexts and 'Kitty' in informal Western contexts, although her official given name is 'Kit Yee'. Similarly, the diagram shows that Janahan Sivakumar should be addressed as 'Mr Janahan' in formal contexts and 'Janahan' in informal contexts. Instructions on how to do this for names from different cultures are provided in part two.

Given name	Middle name	Surname	Preferred name
Kit Yee		Cheung	Kitty
Sivakumar		Janahan	Janahan

Diagram 20: Entering a Cantonese Chinese name and an Indian Tamil name in a databases

When designing a database, I would recommend the following.

- Make sure you include a 'preferred name' field, where you can enter the name the person prefers to use socially. This saves a lot of confusion when someone has chosen to use a nickname or Western name in English-speaking contexts.
- The database should accept a 'surname' only, with nothing entered in the 'given name' field. Many Javanese men have only one name, and this is also found among people from some African countries.
- If you have a separate 'surname' field it should accommodate names of up to at least 18 letters,

especially if you encounter names from Thailand, Sri Lanka or southern India.

- If you have a separate 'given name' field it should accommodate names of up to at least 15 letters and allow you to enter two words with a space between them (e.g. Kit Yee).
- Be careful when using a database to generate address labels or form letters. Names which do not follow the standard Anglo-Saxon structure may not print out correctly.

summary

When communicating directly with someone who has an Asian name, English speakers often find it hard to identify which part of the name should be used to address the person, and how that part of the name should be pronounced. It is also common for English speakers in administrative roles to be confused about how to design the forms and databases into which Asian names are entered. This chapter gives general tips on how to handle these issues, while further details on specific cultures are provided in part two.

part two

introduction
to part two

This section covers names from 14 Asian languages. I have titled the chapters by language of origin (Japanese, Hindi, for instance) rather than country of origin (Japan, India) because names are derived from languages, rather than countries. Also, languages are not used only in their country of origin and more than one language is spoken in most Asian countries. For example, Singapore has four official languages: English, Mandarin, Malay and Tamil.

My first challenge was to decide which Asian languages should be included. Based on the number of speakers and their level of contact with English speakers, I decided to cover the following Asian languages:

- northern Asia: Chinese (Mandarin, Cantonese and Hokkien), Korean, Japanese
- Indo-China: Vietnamese, Thai, Khmer
- southern Asia: Hindi, Tamil, Gurmukhi, Sinhalese, Urdu, Bangla
- South-East Asia: Malay, Indonesian.

The names of India and China, the most highly populated countries in Asia, presented further challenges. There are many Chinese languages and Indian languages from which names may be taken, and I needed to decide whether these languages should be covered as subsections or as separate chapters. As names from different Chinese languages follow the same basic structure, I decided to cover three significant Chinese languages—Mandarin, Cantonese and Hokkien—in a single chapter on Chinese names. As names from different Indian languages have different structures, I decided to devote separate chapters to Hindi, Tamil and Gurmukhi (Sikh) names.

how to use part two

The chapters in part two are organised by language of origin, rather than country of origin. If you need to identify which Asian country a particular name is from, please consult 'Which language is this name from?' (page 213) in part three. If you know the Asian country of origin and need to identify what language it is from, please consult Table 1: Languages spoken in Asian countries on page 211 in part three.

how the chapters are structured

background

This section is divided into two parts: one on the key language or languages of the country, the other on naming customs.

about the language

This touches on the origins of the language, and then focuses on aspects of the language which are relevant for English-speakers using names taken from that language. There is a particular focus on how the language is written, and how words and names in that language are romanised.

about the names

A brief history on how names have been used in that country, and an exploration of how names are chosen and any notable changes in naming customs over time.

structure

Information on what the parts of the name are, and how they are used in different situations.

examples

Two or more examples of names from the language or religious group are provided in this section, with names printed in the original script (if applicable) as well as in romanised form. The different parts of the name are clearly labelled and an explanation of any other details which may be confusing for English speakers is provided.

addressing people

A guide on how to address people in formal and informal situations in an English-speaking context, with the example names as an illustration.

titles

A list of local titles used in that language, explaining what they mean and how they are used.

wives and children

An explanation of how women change their names after marriage, if at all, and what parts of the parents' names, if any, are inherited by children.

anglicising names

How speakers of the language might adapt their name for English-speaking contexts. For example, many speakers of Asian languages may rearrange their names to mimic the 'given name + surname' Anglo-Saxon structure, or adopt a Western name. This section explains how this is usually done by people of that language or religious group.

entering names in a database

This section provides strategies for entering names of the particular Asian language into a database designed for Western names.

pronunciation

Provides guidelines to help English speakers pronounce unfamiliar names. The level of detail given depends on the difficulty of the language being covered. Tables are provided listing vowels, consonants and, in some cases, common combinations of letters, with an explanation of how these should be pronounced in each language.

using the pronunciation tables

These tables provide guidelines for the pronunciation of specific letters and letter combinations.

When the sound represented exists in English, the guidelines provide:

- an English word where the letter is pronounced as it is in the Asian language—see example 1 in Diagram 21
- an example of an English word which contains letters which represent the same sound as in the Asian word—see example 2 in Diagram 21
- providing a combination of letters that give the correct sound if read by an English speaker, as in example 3 in Diagram 21.

When the sound does not exist in English, it is much more difficult to provide guidelines. The methods used in this book include:

- representing the sound in a logical way for English speakers using letters from the Roman alphabet—see example 1 in Diagram 22
- comparing the sound to a word in another European language—see example 2 in Diagram 22
- describing how the unfamiliar sound is produced—see example 3 in Diagram 22.

Example	Letter/s or name	Pronunciation
1	e	As in 'jet'
2	ao	Like 'ow' in 'cow'
3	Linh	Like 'Ln'

Diagram 21: Using the pronunciation tables when a sound exists in English

Example	Letter/s or name	Pronunciation
1	r	Rolled, like the 'r' in Spanish
2	ü	Form the shape of 'oo' with the lips and say 'ee' through them
3	w	Between a 'w' and a 'v'

Diagram 22: Using the pronunciation tables when a sound does not exist in English

pronunciation in different English-speaking countries

People from different English-speaking countries pronounce words in different ways. This is a major problem when using English words to explain pronunciation.

The letter r, for example, poses particular difficulties. In received-pronunciation English, which is spoken in southern Britain, Australia and New Zealand, the r in words like 'churn' and 'car' is not pronounced. For English speakers in these countries, a good way to represent the Cantonese names 'Cheung' and 'Ka' would be 'churng' and 'car' respectively. However, these guidelines would not be effective for English speakers from North America, who pronounce the r in these words.

As far as possible, I have offered guidelines which will work across the major English-speaking countries. In some places, however, you may find that the guidelines are not suited to the dialect of English you speak, so you may need to listen closely to the names and modify them. If in doubt, use the received pronunciation, rather than the North American pronunciation.

which syllable to stress in long names

In English, it is very important to place the stress on the right syllable when saying a word. For example, placing the stress on the first syllable of the word 'desert' makes it a noun meaning 'a dry expanse of land with little vegetation'; placing the stress on the second syllable makes it a verb meaning 'to leave'.

Because of this, English speakers are often concerned about which syllable to stress in long names such as 'Balasubramaniam'. Where possible, the pronunciation guides indicate which syllables should be stressed by putting the stressed syllable in bold type. For example, **Bala**subra**ma**niam.

pronouncing unstressed vowels

The vowels found in syllables which are not stressed, such as the a in 'miracle' or the e in 'mother' are pronounced with the same sound regardless of which vowel they are. In linguistics, this sound is called the *schwa*, and is represented by an upside-down lowercase e (ə).

This sound is common in Asian names, but I didn't want to use a technical symbol to represent it. Instead, I have used the letters uh. In the guides, I have often described this with the phrase 'B says "buh"', alluding to the way children are taught the pronunciation of the letters of the alphabet, as in 'B says buh', 'C says kuh', 'D says duh' and so on.

tones

Names from Chinese languages, Vietnamese, Thai and Punjabi have tones. Tones were explained in detail in chapter 3 (page 28). Although tones are an important part of name pronunciation in these languages, tonal distinctions have not been included in the pronunciation guides. This is because Asian people almost inevitably remove any diacritics which indicate which tones should be used when using their name in an English-speaking context.

aspirated consonants

If you place your hand in front of your lips and say 'top' and then 'stop', you will feel a sharp puff of air on your palm with 'top' but not with 'stop'. This is because the t in the word 'top' is *aspirated*, meaning that there is a breath associated with it. In English, consonants at the start of a word tend to be aspirated, whereas consonants following other letters tend to be unaspirated, as seen in words like 'top' and 'stop', 'kin' and 'skin', 'pat' and 'spat', 'chief' and 'achieve'.

In many Asian languages, both aspirated and unaspirated consonants may be found at the start of a word. For example, a language might contain two different words that sound like 'tip', one in which the t is aspirated, and one in which the t is unaspirated.

When people began romanising Asian languages, they used one of three methods to represent aspirated consonants. These methods are outlined below.

- Placing an h after the aspirated consonant to symbolise a puff of air—that is, a word with the aspirated t is spelt 'thip' and a word with an unaspirated t is spelt 'tip'. This system was used in south Asia and Indo-China. The disadvantage of this method is that it is often misleading. For example, English speakers will probably pronounce th in the way it sounds in the word 'thin', and ph as an f sound.
- Placing an apostrophe after the aspirated consonant—using this system, the word with the aspirated t is spelt 't'ip' and the word with the unaspirated t is spelt 'tip'. This system was used in east Asia. The disadvantage of this method is that the apostrophe breaks up the syllable and its meaning is not clear. Such apostrophes are commonly omitted from names for everyday use. For example, the capital of Taiwan should in theory be written T'aipei, but is usually written Taipei. Another problem is that apostrophes often cause difficulties with computers, which often do not accept punctuation marks in the middle of web addresses, document titles and so on.
- Using different letters to represent unaspirated and aspirated consonants—for example, the word with the aspirated t would be spelt 'tip' and the word with the unaspirated t would be spelt 'dip', as a b sound is similar to the sound of an unaspirated p—although

the sound of a **d** is not exactly the same as the sound of an unaspirated **t**. This method has been used since about 1950 and is now preferred because it provides a clear guide to pronunciation for uninformed readers and people who work with computer systems.

The table below shows the different ways in which the most common aspirated and unaspirated consonants are represented.

As explained in this book	Using 'h'	Using apostrophe	Using different letters
Aspirated ch as in 'chief'	chh	ch'	ch
Unaspirated ch, as in 'achieve'	ch	ch	j
Aspirated k, as in 'kin'	kh	k'	k
Unaspirated k, as in 'skin'	k	k	g
Aspirated p, as in 'pin'	ph	p'	p
Unaspirated p, as in 'spin'	p	p	b
Aspirated t, as in 'top'	th	t'	t
Unaspirated t, as in 'stop'	t	t	d

Diagram 23: Different ways common consonants are represented

common names

This section lists common names for each language. Where applicable, there is also information about how to distinguish male and female given names, which names were popular during different eras, and how to pronounce particularly common names.

chapter 5
Chinese
names

background

about the languages of China

There is no single language called Chinese. When people in English-speaking countries refer to 'Chinese', they usually mean either *Mandarin*, the official national language of China, or *Cantonese*, the most widely spoken language among the people of Chinese ethnicity who live outside China. There are in fact many more languages which have their origins in China and are part of the Sino-Tibetan language family to which Mandarin and Cantonese belong. These languages are often referred to informally as Chinese *dialects*, and this term will be used here for the sake of clarity. Many linguists, however, argue that they should be referred to as Chinese *languages* instead, because they are not mutually intelligible. A monolingual Mandarin speaker, for example, would not be able to understand spoken Cantonese and vice versa.

Chinese languages are written using a logographical system (see page 18) known to English speakers as 'Chinese characters'. The same set of characters is used to write all Chinese languages (albeit with some regional variation in grammar and vocabulary), despite the fact that they sound different in spoken form. In most cases, a particular character means the same thing to any literate speaker of any Chinese language, but the way it is pronounced differs depending on the language in which it is read aloud.

A good way of understanding how this works is to look at Arabic numerals. For example, although the symbol 3 means the same thing all over Europe, it is pronounced **three** in English, **trois** in French, **drei** in German and so on. Similarly, the symbol 王 represents a common family name all over China, but is pronounced differently in different regions. Because of this, the Mandarin pronunciation of this name is romanised as **Wang**, the Cantonese pronunciation as **Wong**, and the Hokkien pronunciation as **Ong**.

Symbol	Pronunciation		
3	**English** Three	**French** Trois	**German** Drei
王	**Mandarin** Wang	**Cantonese** Wong	**Hokkien** Ong

This chapter covers the three Chinese languages English speakers are most likely to encounter, namely Mandarin, Cantonese and Hokkien. Note that these languages are also known by different names, as explained shortly.

Although speakers of these three languages pronounce and spell Chinese characters in different ways, their names follow the same basic structure. Because of this, these languages are covered in a single chapter, rather than as separate chapters.

Mandarin

Mandarin is the official national language of China and Taiwan, and one of the four official languages of Singapore (the other three are English, Malay and Tamil). In China, it is usually called pútōnghùa, which means 'common speech', although you may also hear it called hànyǔ (usually refers to speech), or zhōngwén (usually refers to written language). Mandarin is often referred to as guǒyǔ in Taiwan and húayǔ in Malaysia and Singapore.

Mandarin developed from the standard language used by scholars and officials during the Ming dynasty (1368–1644) and Qing dynasty (1644–1912). It spread easily across the northern plains of China, but was prevented by mountainous terrain from extending too far into southern China. As the language of the educated elite, spoken in the capital city and across much of the country, Mandarin was suggested as a national language after China became a republic in 1912, and was officially declared to be the national language shortly after the Communist party came to power in 1949.

A number of language reforms were applied to Mandarin in China during the 1950s and 1960s. Several hundred commonly used Chinese characters were simplified, with the aim of raising literacy in the general population. For example, the character jian, meaning 'to see', was simplified from 見 to 见. These simplified characters are officially used in China and have been adopted in Singapore, though the traditional, more complex forms are still used in other Chinese societies. Even in China and Singapore, unsimplified characters are still used in some contexts, as they are considered to be more elegant and traditional.

Another significant reform in China was the adoption of a new official system of romanisation called hànyǔ pīnyīn. The most commonly used romanisation system prior to this reform was the Wade–Giles system, in which Chairman Mao's full name is written **Mao Tse-Tung**, and apostrophes are used to indicate aspirated consonants (see page 60), as in **Ch'ing** dynasty. In the hànyǔ pīnyīn system, these names are written **Mao Zedong** and **Qing**. Wade–Giles romanisation is still used for Mandarin in Taiwan and is seen commonly in Western print media, leading to confusion when people see the names of people and places being spelt in different ways.

Characters	毛泽东	清
Wade–Giles romanisation	Mao Tse-Tung	Ch'ing
Hànyǔ pīnyīn romanisation	Mao Zedong	Qing

Cantonese

Cantonese originates from the city of Guangzhou, the capital of Guangdong, the southern Chinese province first known to the West as 'Canton'. In China this language is called guǎngdōnghuà. Cantonese is still spoken as a first language in Hong Kong and Guangdong, and is the most commonly spoken language among the Chinese who live outside China. This is because of the many Chinese who emigrated from China in the 19th and early 20th centuries; the Cantonese were the most numerous and travelled the furthest, with many eventually settling in English-speaking countries. For this reason, up until around the 1990s, almost all of the 'Chinese' food available in Western countries was Cantonese food.

Most Cantonese write in unsimplified characters, rather than the simplified characters devised by the Chinese government in the 1950s. Even in Guangdong, where people are officially meant to use simplified characters, traditional characters are most often used on signs. In Singapore, however, where there are many Cantonese speakers, simplified characters have officially been adopted.

In Hong Kong, where Cantonese is an official language, a number of competing romanisation systems have been used, leading to a range of different romanised spellings for the same Cantonese words and names. There is now an official system used by the Hong Kong government for registering personal names and place names. However, in many cases Hong Kong people have continued to use established spellings rather than changing to the government system.

Outside Hong Kong, Cantonese speakers do not apply any consistent romanisation system.

Hokkien

Hokkien has its origins in the south-eastern Chinese province of Fújìan, in which it is the language spoken in regions south of the Min River. Hokkien is also spoken in Taiwan, where it is often referred to as 'Taiwanese'.

In Mandarin, the name for this language is **Mǐnnánhùa** ('Min south speech'). Many of the Chinese living in Singapore, Malaysia and Indonesia are Hokkien speakers.

Hokkien is not an official language in any country, and there is no widely accepted romanisation system, though in Taiwan a system developed by Presbyterian missionaries called **Péh-ōe-jī** may be used.

about Chinese names

Chinese names traditionally comprise three characters, of which the first is the 'family name', the second is usually the 'generation name' and the third is usually the 'personal name'. As described in chapter 3, this is the classic Confucian name structure, and illustrates the family-centred, hierarchical philosophy which Confucius espoused.

Chinese family names are inherited down the paternal line, like English surnames. The great majority of these family names consist of a single character. Although several hundred family names exist, almost 60 per cent of Chinese people have one of the 20 most common family names.

The generation name is shared by siblings of the same sex in the same generation. For example, my mother's name is Chan Gim Luan, and her three sisters are called Chan Gim Phaik, Chan Gim Hong and Chan Gim Lin. The generation name is usually placed second in Chinese names, though in a minority of cases it may be placed third. Since about the 1960s, the use of generation names has been declining in Mainland China. A strong minority of Mainland Chinese now have two character names containing only a family name and a personal name, for example Zhou Ming (周明). Among the Chinese living overseas, however, including a generation name remains the norm.

Some very traditional families may have a generation name poem. The generation names of the sons in the family are taken from the characters of this poem. That is, the children in the first generation are given the first character in the poem as a generation name, their children use the second character in the poem, and so on. When the end of the poem is reached, the family either extends the poem further, or returns to the top of the poem and starts again.

Personal names (and in most cases generation names) are traditionally chosen by the father's side of the family, notably the paternal grandfather. In recent decades, however, the influence of the mother and other family members has been growing. The meaning of the characters is very important when choosing a child's name. Boys are typically named after 'masculine' attributes, like courage, success, diligence and intelligence, or large fierce animals, like dragons and tigers. Girls are more likely to be named after 'feminine' qualities, such as beauty, gentleness and grace, or flowers, seasons and precious stones.

Various other factors may also be taken into account. Some families might avoid choosing a name which would bring the total number of strokes in the names to a number ending in four, as the number four sounds like the word for 'death' in many Chinese languages. They might also consult the elements associated with the hour, day, month and year of birth in the child's astrological chart and choose a name which corrects any imbalance. For example, if the child's chart was lacking in wood, a name containing 木, the symbol for wood, could be chosen to balance the deficiency.

structure

examples of Chinese names

There are regional differences in the way romanised Chinese names are written. In Mainland China, names contain two components when written correctly using the hànyǔ pīnyīn system. When the name contains three characters, as seen in the example Ye Jianping, the generation name and personal name are written together as a single two-syllable word. This is also the case for names containing two characters (e.g. Liu Jia) and the rare names that contain four characters (e.g. Ouyang Renrong). The diacritical marks on Yè Jīanpíng indicate the tones with which these syllables are pronounced. Chinese people usually remove these marks when they leave China as they are unlikely to be understood by foreigners. For this reason, they will be omitted from the name in the rest of this chapter.

		Family name	Generation name	Personal name
Female Hokkien (Malaysian Chinese)	Characters	鄭	美	雲
	Romanised	Tay	Bee	Yun
Male Mandarin (Mainland China)	Characters	叶	剑 平	
	Romanised	Yè	Jiànpíng	
Female Cantonese (Hong Kong)	Characters	張	淑	蓮
	Romanised	Cheung	Suk	Lin

Outside China, the three characters are usually romanised as three separate components. In Taiwan, and among Chinese people born in Western countries, people sometimes place a hyphen between the generation name and given name (e.g. Chao Shu-Ling).

addressing Chinese people

The standard way to address Chinese people in English-speaking contexts is title + family name for formal address, and generation name + personal name for informal address. Note that the Chinese commonly adapt the name they use for informal address in English-speaking countries. Many adopt a Western name, or use just one of their three characters socially. For example, Bee Yun might decide to call herself 'Yun' to make her name easier to pronounce and remember. It is also not uncommon for men from Mainland China to use only their family name for address when overseas.

The Mainland Chinese who have only two characters in their names (e.g. Zhou Ming) typically use both of them for informal address.

	Formal address	Informal address
Female Hokkien	Ms Tay	Bee Yun
Male Mandarin	Mr Ye	Jianping
Female Cantonese	Ms Cheung	Suk Lin

Chinese titles

Mandarin titles

Commonly used titles in Mandarin include the informal **Xiao** and **Lao**. These are used among colleague and classmates; the other more formal titles are listed in the table below. **Xiao** and **Lao** are placed before the family name; for example, Ye Jianping could be addressed as **Xiao Ye** or **Lao Ye**. **Xiao** (which literally means 'little') is used for addressing people who are younger or of equal to lower status than the speaker; **Lao** ('old') is used for people who are older or of higher status.

The other titles listed in the table can be used on their own. A doctor could be addressed simply as **Daifu**, for instance. Otherwise, the titles are placed after the family name. If addressing Ye Jianping in a formal context, the equivalent of Mr Ye would be Ye Xiansheng.

Note that the use of titles seems to change quickly in China. **Tongzhi**, which means 'comrade' and was once commonly used as a unisex title, is now more often used as slang for a homosexual person. The title **Xiaojie**, once widely used to address female service staff and young women, is now being used as a slang term for a prostitute. **Taitai**, sometimes abbreviated to just **Tai**, is also rather dated, and now has the connotation of an old, rich woman.

Title	English equivalent	Title	English equivalent
Xiansheng	Mr	Xiao	literally 'little'
Taitai	Madam/Mrs (older woman)	Lao	literally 'old'
Xiaojie	Miss (younger woman)	Daifu	Doctor (medical)
Nüshi	Ms	Boshi	Doctor (PhD)

Cantonese titles

As with Cantonese names, Cantonese titles may be romanised in various ways. Where two romanisations are provided, separated by a comma, in the table below, the first is taken from a Cantonese–English dictionary compiled by Parker Po-Fei Huang and the second is a common colloquial variant.

Title	English equivalent	Title	English equivalent
A, Ah	–	Zai	–
Sinsaang, Sinsan	Mr	Luisee	Ms
TaaiTaai,Taitai (or just Taai,Tai)	Madam/Mrs for an older woman	Yisang, Yeesan	Doctor (medical)
Siuje, Siuche	Miss	Lousih, Losee	Teacher (also for academics)

The title **Ah** has no English equivalent. **Ah** is most often placed before the personal name, as in **Ah Lin**, before the family name, as in **Ah Cheung**, or before generation name + personal name, as in **Ah Suk Lin**. This form of address is generally used in an affectionate or friendly manner with friends or family members.

Zai is an affectionate diminutive used for addressing small boys or a man who is much younger than the speaker, and is usually placed after the personal name.

The other Cantonese titles listed are formal, and are typically placed after the family name, e.g. Cheung Yeesan. Note, however, that Chinese titles are seldom used among Chinese people living overseas—outside China and Hong Kong, English titles or the titles of the country of residence are typically used.

Hokkien titles

Because Hokkien is not the official language of any country, it is seldom used in formal contexts and survives primarily as a spoken language used among friends, family members and for trade among locals in Hokkien-speaking regions. As a result, the titles shown below are seldom used. Where two romanisations, separated by a comma, are provided, the first is from the *Taiwanhua Dictionary* and the second is a common colloquial variant (to superscript n in 'Sin-se[n]' means that the sound should be nasalised without pronouncing the n).

The titles are placed after the family name (Tay I-seng), or used by themselves in a similar way to 'Sir' and 'Madam'. The almost obsolete Seohchia may also be used after generation name + personal name.

The southern Chinese title Ah is also used by Hokkien speakers, and is explained above under Cantonese titles.

Title	English equivalent	Title	English equivalent
Sin-se[n], Sinseh	Mr, teacher	I-seng, Yeeseng	Doctor (medical)
Tai-tai	Mrs (old fashioned)	Phok-su	Doctor (PhD)
Sio-chia, Seohchia	Miss (very formal)		

wives and children

In Chinese-speaking contexts, women do not usually change their names after marriage. However, in an English-speaking context, Chinese women are often happy to be addressed informally by 'Mrs' followed by their husband's family name. For example, if Bee Yun and Jianping were to marry, Bee Yun would not change her official name. However, she might not mind being addressed informally as 'Mrs Ye', although it would be wise to ask, as she might prefer Ms Tay.

Children take their father's family name.

anglicising Chinese names

The Chinese commonly adapt their names for use in English-speaking contexts. The two main ways in which they do this are shown in the example below.

Name in original Chinese order	Family name	Generation name	Personal name
	Cheung	Suk	Lin
1. Rearranged into Western order	**Given name**	**Middle name**	**Surname**
	Suk Lin		Cheung
2. Adding a Western name	**Given name**	**Middle name**	**Surname**
	Angelina	(Suk Lin)	Cheung

Using method 1, people with Chinese names simply shift their family name to the end, so that their names reflect the standard Western given name + surname order.

In method 2, people with Chinese names (including

most people from Mainland China) adopt a Western given name, which they use with their family name (e.g. Angelina Cheung, William Ye). The generation name and personal name are either left out informally or entered as a middle name.

entering Chinese names in a database

When entering a Chinese name into a Western database, the family name should *always* be placed under 'surname'. The generation name and personal name should *both* be placed under 'given name', whether they are hyphenated together, as seen in Taiwan (Chiang Kai-Shek), separate (Tay Bee Yun) or written together as a two-syllable word (Ye Jianping). For two character Mainland Chinese names with no generation name present, the second component of the name should be entered under 'given name'.

The above instructions apply when the name is written in traditional Chinese order. However, if the person has Westernised their name, they may have placed the family name last to imitate the Anglo-Saxon given name + surname structure. This can make it difficult to determine which part of the name is the family name (unless the generation name and personal name are either hyphenated or joined together to form a two-syllable name). If you are not sure whether the name has been Westernised or not, contact the person and ask.

If a Western name is present, the name can be entered in one of two ways, depending on whether the name is an official name—used in the person's passport and other important documents—or an assumed name they picked up for convenience. In Example 1 below, 'Sally' is the official given name, and should be entered under 'given name', with the generation and personal names entered together under 'middle name'. In Example 2, 'Sally' is an assumed name, and should be entered under 'preferred name', with the generation name and personal name entered under 'given name'. Again, if you are not sure which option is best, ask the person.

	Given name	Middle name	Surname	Preferred name
Example 1	Sally	Bee Yun	Tay	
Example 2	Bee Yun		Tay	Sally

pronunciation: Mandarin

Mandarin names are romanised using the hanyu pinyin system in Mainland China. In Taiwan, the Wade–Giles system is typically used, although the Taiwanese sometimes omit the apostrophes that indicate aspirated consonants (see introduction to part two) in the Wade–Giles system. In Singapore, there is no official romanisation system.

consonants

Consonants used in hanyu pinyin that are not pronounced as they are in English are listed in the table on the next page, followed by their equivalent in the Wade–Giles system. For example, the character 邱 would be romanised as Qiu in China, where the hanyu pinyin system is used, and as Ch'iu in Taiwan, where the Wade–Giles system is used.

success with Asian names

Hanyu pinyin (Mainland China)	Wade–Giles (Taiwan)	Pronunciation
c	ts'	Like 'ts' in 'bits'
q	ch'	Like 'ch' in 'cheese'
r	j	Like an English 'r' with the tongue curled behind the front teeth, as it is when saying 'pleasure'
x	hs	Similar to the 'sh' in 'shin'
z	ts	Like the 'dz' in 'adze'
zh	ch	Like the 'j' in 'jet'

vowels

a	As in 'father'		o	Like 'aw' in 'paw'
e	As in 'Bert' (except 'ye', which is as in 'yet')		u	As in 'put' (for xu, yu, qu, ju; *see below*)
i	Like 'ee' in 'bee' (for si, shi, ci, chi, zi, zhi, ri; *see below*)		ü	Like 'u' in the French 'tu' (lips form 'oo', say 'ee')
i	Like 'uh' (e.g. 'B says buh')			

endings

ai	As in 'aisle'		ang	Like 'ung' in 'hung'
an	As in 'Khan'		ao	Like 'ow' in 'cow'

ei	Like the 'ay' in 'jay'	ong	As if written 'oong', with 'oo' as in 'book'
en	Like 'e' in 'fern' followed by n	ou	Like the 'o' in 'Jo'
eng	Like 'e' in 'fern' followed by ng	ua	As in 'guava'
er	Between the 'ur' in 'blur' and the 'ar' in 'car'	uai	Like the word 'why'
ia	'ee' in 'bee' plus 'a' in 'father'	uan	'oo' as in 'moo', plus 'an' as in 'Khan' (or 'en' as in 'ten' for juan, quan, xuan and yuan)
ian	'ee' in 'bee' plus 'en' in 'ten'	uang	Like 'wung', to rhyme with 'lung'
iang	'ee' in 'bee' plus 'ung' in 'lung'	ue	Like the word 'wear' (don't pronounce the final 'r')
iao	'ee' in 'bee' plus 'ow' in 'cow'	ui	Like the word 'way'
ie	'ee' in 'bee' plus 'e' in 'get'	un	'u' as in 'put' (for xun, qun, jun, yun; see below)
iong	'ee' in 'bee' plus oong ('oo' as in 'book')	ün	'u' as in the French 'tu' followed by 'n'
iu	'ee' in 'bee' plus 'o' in 'Jo'	uo	'oo' as in 'moo' plus 'aw' in 'paw'

common Mandarin names

The tables below show ten of the most common Chinese family names, and twelve syllables commonly used as generation names or personal names. The hanyu pinyin spelling is placed first, with the Wade–Giles spelling placed after it in parentheses if it is different.

family names

Family name	Approximate pronunciation	Family name	Approximate pronunciation
Chen (Ch'en)	Like the word 'churn', with RP pronunciation*	Wang	Wahng (to rhyme with 'lung')
Huang	Hwahng (to rhyme with 'lung')	Wu	Woo
Li	Lee	Yang	Like the word "young"
Lin	Lin	Zhang (Chang)	Jahng (to rhyme with 'lung')
Liu	Leo	Zhou (Chou)	Joe

* For North Americans, 'chun' to rhyme with 'bun' will be a closer approximation

generation and person names

The following names are commonly used as either generation names or personal names. The list is organised in alphabetical order by the hanyu pinyin romanisations used in China. If the Wade–Giles romanisation is different, it follows in parentheses. For example, the character 小 would be romanised as 'Xiao' in China, whereas in Taiwan the same character would be romanised as 'Hsiao'.

Name	Approximate pronunciation	Name	Approximate pronunciation
Hui	As if spelled 'Hway'	Wei	Way
Jia (Chia)	Jee-ah	Wen	'Wurn' (to rhyme with 'burn') with RP pronunciation*
Jie (Chieh)	Jee-eh	Xiao (Hsiao)	Shee-ow ('ow' as in "cow")
Mei	May	Yan	Yan (to rhyme with 'pan')
Qing (Ch'ing)	Ching	Zhao (Chao)	Jow (to rhyme with 'cow')
Shi (Shih)	Shr	Zi (Tzu)	Zuh (as in "Z says zuh"

*For North Americans, 'wun' to rhyme with 'bun' will be a closer approximation.

pronunciation: Cantonese and Hokkien names

It is difficult to write a pronunciation guide for names in Cantonese and Hokkien as these languages do not have a clear and well-established romanisation system. In many cases, the way a Chinese name is romanised for Chinese children born outside China depends on the whim of the registrar, and may be a poor representation of its actual sound. This is further complicated by the tendency of Chinese people living overseas to Westernise the pronunciation of their names.

consonants

The way consonants are pronounced can vary from name to name.

g	Hard, as in 'girl' (not soft, as in 'gel')	th	Like 't' in 'tack'
hs	Between 's' and 'sh'	ts	Like 'ts' in 'bits'
ng	Like the 'ng' in 'sing'	x	Between 's' and 'sh'

vowels

a	As in 'father'	o	Either 'o' as in 'toe' or 'or' as in 'bore'
e	As in 'her'	u	As in 'put' (or rarely as in 'luck')
i	Like 'ee' in 'bee'		

endings

ai	As in 'aisle'	ia, eah	'ee-**ah**' (e.g. Hsia, Cheah)
au	'ow' as in 'cow' (e.g. Lau)	iau, iao	'ee-**ow**' (ow as in 'cow')
eat	Between 'ee-**att**' and 'ee-**utt**' (e.g. Keat)	iu	'ee-**oo**' (e.g. Liu)
ei	As in 'weigh' (e.g. Mei, Fei, Lei)	ua	'wah' (e.g. Huan, Fua)
eung	e in 'fern' followed by 'ng' (e.g. Leung, Cheung)	un	With u as in 'put'

common names in Cantonese and Hokkien

If the common Mandarin, Cantonese and Hokkien names listed in this chapter were written in Chinese characters as well as in romanised form, you would see that many family names in fact appear on all three lists. However, as explained previously, the same character tends to be pronounced differently in different Chinese dialects. As a result, the romanised versions of the name look completely different. For example, the character 吳 is a common family name throughout China, and it appears in all three lists. In Mandarin, it is romanised as 'Wu', in Cantonese as 'Ng' and in Hokkien it is usually 'Goh'.

For pronunciation of these common Cantonese and Hokkien names, see previous page.

family names

Cantonese	Chan, Chang, Cheung, Chow, Ho, Lam, Lau, Lee, Ng, Wong, Yip
Hokkien	Chew, Goh, Khoo, Lim, Looi, Neoh, Ong, Ooi, Tay, Teo, Yap, Yeo

generation and personal names

Cantonese		Hokkien	
Name	Approximate pronunciation	**Name**	Approximate pronunication
Man	'mun' (rhyming with 'bun')	Bee	Like the English word 'bee'
Mei	'may'	Gim	'G' as in 'gift', rhyming with 'Jim'

success with Asian names

Siew	'see' followed by 'ew' in 'few'	Heng	As written, 'e' as in 'hen'
Suk	'sook' (rhyming with 'book')	Keat	'kee' followed by 'ut' in 'hut'
Wai	Like the word 'why'	Soo	Like the word 'sue'

chapter 6
Korean
names

background

about the Korean language

Korean is the official language of both North Korea and South Korea. It was written using Chinese characters, which the Koreans refer to as *hanja*, until the middle of the 15th century, when King Sejong of the Chosŭn dynasty invented the alphabet used today. This alphabet is called *hangeul* (or *hangŭl*) in the south, where hanja are still seen and taught, and *Chosŏngŭl* in the north, where the use of hanja is banned. Unlike words written in the Roman alphabet, where letters are placed next to one another and ordered from left to right, letters in Korean words (called *jamo*) are arranged together into a rectangular-shaped box, as seen on page 26 and in the examples that follow.

Most Korean people use the McCune–Reischauer system of romanisation developed in 1937. This system uses diacritics to modify the sounds of letters. For example, it places a *breve* over the letter u (ŭ) to change its sound from the oo in 'book' to the eu in the French word feu. It also inserts apostrophes to distinguish between aspirated consonants and unaspirated consonants.

In 2000, the National Academy of the Korean Language developed a new system called the Revised Romanization System. This system avoids the use of apostrophes and diacritics, which make words difficult to enter into a computer. The Revised Romanization System inserts an e instead of putting a breve over the vowel, hence hangeul rather than hangŭl, and avoids apostrophes by using g/k, d/t and b/p (to distinguish unaspirated/aspirated consonants—see page 60) to replace k/k', t/t' and p/p'. For example, the words kim and k'im in the McCune–Reischauer system are written as gim and kim in the Revised Romanization System.

Although signs around Korea are in the process of being changed to the Revised Romanization System, for personal names most people are keeping established spellings. The examples below show the hangeul for five common Korean family names with the most common romanisation (usually based on the McCune–Reischauer system), the new Revised Romanization System, and other romanisations which you may see.

Family names in hangeul	Most common romanisation	Revised Romanization System	Other possible romanisations
김	Kim	Gim	
이	Lee	I	Rhee, Ri, Yi
박	Park	Bak	Pak
정	Chung	Jeong	Chong
최	Choi	Choe	

about Korean names

Many centuries ago, the Korean people had indigenous names which typically consisted of a single given name, often three syllables in length. Under the influence of the Chinese, they began adopting family names between one and two thousand years ago. Most Korean names today follow the classic Confucian structure (see page 35), with a family name, generation name and personal name.

Between 1910 and 1945, Korea was occupied by Japan. During this period, people were pressured to adopt Japanese family names or to pronounce their family name hanja in Japanese, and many girls received given names ending in 子, which is pronounced -ja in Korean and -ko in Japanese. In 1946, the Japanese were defeated, and the Name Restoration Order allowed Koreans to readopt their original names.

In Korea, names are traditionally chosen by the paternal grandparents, or the oldest living relatives on the father's side, with men's input being weighted more heavily than women's. More recently, this has begun to change, with parents and women having more say about what their child will be called.

Until the 1970s or so, names were usually registered in hanja. Since then, however, more and more children have been registered under hangeul-only names, as a patriotic gesture. Even people who have a hanja name on their birth certificate commonly use only hangeul in their daily life. For example, Kim Myong Mee's birth certificate might read 金 明 美, but she would probably only ever write her name in hangeul, 김 명 미. You may also occasionally see people from devoutly Christian families with Biblical names rendered in hangeul, like Da Ni Eul (다 니 을 Daniel).

structure

examples of Korean names

Like Chinese names, Korean names typically contain three one-syllable components, of which the first is the family name. The remaining two parts are traditionally the generation name and personal name. Most Korean families swap the positions of the generation name and personal name each generation. That is, if one generation places the names in the order family name, generation name + personal name, the next generation will order them family name, personal name + generation name. Note, however, that Korean parents are increasingly picking two names according to personal preference rather than following the strict generation-name tradition.

		Family name	Personal name	Generation name
Female	Hangeul	김	명	미
	romanised	Kim	Myong	Mee
		Family name	Generation name	Personal name
Male	Hangeul	초	체	현
	romanised	Cho	Chae	Hyeon

Although officially Koreans write their names in three separate one-syllable components, you may also see people hyphenating their generation name and personal name (Kim Myong-Mee, Cho Chae-Hyeon) or combining their generation name and personal name into a single two-syllable word (e.g. Kim Myongmee, Cho Chaehyeon). There is also a small but growing number of Koreans who have only a family name and personal name.

addressing Korean people

	Formal address	Informal address
Female	Ms Kim	Myong Mee
Male	Mr Cho	Chae Hyeon

Korean titles

The use of titles in Korean is very complex, and is closely linked to relative status and age. In addition to the general titles explained in the table below, Koreans also have a range of titles used in business (e.g. President; sajang), which are placed after the family name and refer to a person's position in the company (e.g. Cho Sajang).

McCune–Reischauer system	Revised Romanization System	Comments
ssi	ssi	Unisex general title, equivalent to Mr/Ms, used among people of similar age and status. Placed after the given name it is informal; placed after the family name it is formal and implies that the speaker is of higher status

McCune–Reischauer system	Revised Romanization System	Comments
sŏnsaengnim	seonsaengnim	Formal title used to show respect to older people (male or female), used alone or placed after the family name or full name
samonim	samonim	Formal title used to show respect to a married woman. Used by itself or following family name
yŏsa	yeosa	Very formal title, seldom used. For married women of very high status, used with the family name or full name
ajŏssi	ajeossi	Literally means 'uncle'. Used informally for older men in informal contexts. Ssi often precedes it, e.g. Park Ssi Ajŏssi
ajumma	ajumma	Used for older married women, Park See Ajumma, or just by itself
kun	gun	Formal title, seldom used. For boys and men much younger than the speaker, placed after the family name or given name
yang	yang	Formal title, seldom used. For unmarried girls and women much younger than the speaker, placed after the family name or given name

wives and children

In Korea, women do not change their family name after marriage. However, in an English-speaking country, Korean women may follow local custom and use Mrs with their husband's family name. Occasionally the husband and wife may combine their family names after marriage, placing the man's name first e.g. 'Chokim'.

Children take their father's family name unless their parents have adopted a combined family name, like Chokim, in which case they will inherit this instead.

anglicising Korean names

In English-speaking contexts, Korean people typically use generation name + personal name, the part they are known by informally, as a 'given name', and their family name as a 'surname'. This adaptation gives their names an Anglo-Saxon structure, and helps English speakers to address them correctly. They may also combine their generation and personal names into a single two-syllable word, to ensure that both are used together.

	Given name	Surname
Female	Myong Mee (or Myongmee)	Kim
Male	Chae Hyeon (or Chaehyeon)	Cho

entering Korean names in a database

When entering a Korean name into a Western database, place the family name in the 'surname' field, and the generation and personal names in the 'given name' field in the original order. Do *not* enter the generation name under 'middle name'.

Occasionally, a Korean person may use a Western name. For example, if Kim Myong Mee was born in the United States, her parents might have decided to include an official Western name, 'Tina', on her birth certificate. Alternatively, Kim Myong Mee might have decided to adopt the name Tina informally while studying in the United States.

If Tina is an official name, it should be entered under 'given name', with the generation name and personal name *both* entered under 'middle name', as shown in Example 1. If Tina is an assumed name, it should be entered under 'preferred name', with the generation name and personal name *both* entered under 'given name', as shown in Example 2.

	Given name	Middle name	Surname	Preferred name
Example 1	Tina	Myong Mee	Kim	
Example 2	Myong Mee		Kim	Tina

pronunciation

consonants

Consonants in Korean are generally pronounced as they are in English. However, English speakers may be confused to note that the initial consonant in names like Chae and Park sound more like j and b than ch and p. This is because the ch and p are unaspirated. That is, they are not pronounced with the harsh exhalation of air you hear when these sounds are at the start of a word in English (as in **pin**) but in the gentler way they are pronounced when these sounds are later in the word (as in **spin**).

In the McCune–Reischauer system, aspirated consonants are marked with an apostrophe (e.g. the sound of the English **pin** would be written **p'in**), but these apostrophes tend to be left out when Koreans write their names in the Roman alphabet.

vowels

a	As in 'father'	ŭi	u in 'fur' followed by ee in 'bee'
ae	Like a in 'care'	wa	'wah', to rhyme with 'ma'
e	As in 'jet'	wae	Like 'wear' without pronouncing the r
eo	Like the word 'awe'	we	Like the 'we' in 'wet'
i	Like ee in 'bee'	wi	Like the word 'we'
o	As in 'go'	ya	As in 'yard'
u	As in 'put'	ye	As in 'yet'
ŭ, eu	Like the 'u' in 'fur'	yo	Like 'yaw' in 'yawn'

common Korean family names

The pronunciations below represent the way these names are pronounced in Korean. When speaking in English, these family names are usually pronounced exactly the way they would be in English in the case of Kim, Lee and Park; Choong (with the oo as in 'book') for Chung; Cho to rhyme with 'no'; and Choi to rhyme with 'boy'. Most Koreans quickly adapt to this.

Name	Pronunciation	Name	Approximate pronunciation
Kim	Gim	Chung	'Je' in 'jet' followed by 'ong'
Lee	Ee	Cho	Like 'chaw'
Park	Buck	Choi	'J' sound followed by the 'we' in 'wet'

common Korean generation and personal names

The table below offers examples of generation or personal names which were popular in different eras for Korean men and women. Of course, these eras are not absolute and there are examples of some names being used across different eras. Note that there may be alternative spellings for many of these names. For example, 'Ju' may also be spelt 'Joo'.

Era	Men	Women
pre–1960	Chae, Cheol, Hee, Pyong, Suk, Tae, Woo	Chun, Ja (always placed on the end, e.g. Jeong Ja), Jeong, Kŭm, Yeong
1960–90	Hee, Ho, Hyun, Seong, Song, Suk	Hee, Jee, Ju, Mee, Moon, Myong, Sook, Yung
1990s onwards	Gyu, Ho, Kang, Min, Sang, Woo	Bee, Eun, Jin, Su, Ta, Won

chapter 7
Japanese names

background

about the Japanese language

The national language of Japan is Japanese. Although Japanese has borrowed much of its vocabulary from Chinese and shares grammatical similarities with Korean, it is generally believed to be in a language family of its own. It uses a combination of three different writing systems: *kanji*, *hiragana* and *katakana*.

Kanji are the characters the Japanese have borrowed from the Chinese over the centuries, and are a logographic writing system (see page 18). In Japanese, a single character may have several pronunciations. Despite the use of symbols borrowed from the Chinese, the Japanese and Chinese languages are not thought to be related, as they have very different grammar.

Hiragana and katakana are syllabaries (see page 20). Just as each of the 26 letters in the Roman alphabet can be written with either a capital letter or a lowercase letter, the 70 or so syllables in the Japanese language can be written with either a hiragana symbol or a katakana symbol (e.g. the symbol for ta is written た in hiragana and タ in katakana). Hiragana tend to be curved and curly and are used for native Japanese words; katakana tend to be pointy and angular, and are used for imported foreign words.

Over time, some *kana* (a word referring to symbols from either syllabary) have become obsolete, and new symbols have been introduced to represent sounds not present in Japanese. For example, Japanese has no v sound, but a new symbol has been developed to represent the v sound for words borrowed from English. Nonetheless, as you become familiar with Japanese names, you will note that certain syllables come up again and again.

Japanese is usually romanised using a revised version of the Hepburn system, which was originally published in 1867 by the American missionary Reverend James Hepburn. This system was designed as a pronunciation guide for English speakers, and is generally a logical guide to the way names sound. See the section on pronunciation for further details.

about Japanese names

Up until the mid-19th century, ordinary Japanese people had only one name, as family names were considered the preserve of royalty and samurai. However, after the Meiji Restoration in 1868, commoners began adopting family names, partly because it was at this point in history that the Japanese began to register births, deaths and marriages.

Japanese parents usually choose their children's names themselves. Buddhist families may choose to consult a monk as well, though this practice is now rare. Family names are always written in kanji; given names may be written in kanji or hiragana or a combination of the two. Hiragana given names are more popular among women, as they are considered feminine.

Given names are chosen based on a combination of their meaning, the way they sound, and how well they combine with the family name. In the past few decades, sound has become the most important issue for most Japanese parents when selecting names. Traditionally, however, parents considered it equally important to ensure that the total number of strokes in a child's name was an auspicious number, and that there was a good balance of the five elements (water, wood, fire, metal and earth) in the name. For example, parents with the family name Morita (森田), meaning 'forest rice-field', would not want to call their son Naoki (直樹), meaning 'straight tree', because the overall name would contain too many characters containing the symbol for wood (木).

structure

examples of Japanese names

Japanese people have a family name and a given name. The family name is usually composed of one to three kanji, most often two, and the given name is usually composed of one or two kanji, most often two. You may occasionally see given names written in hiragana rather than kanji, especially for girls (as hiragana are considered to be feminine). For example, 'Sakura', meaning cherry blossom, might be written in hiragana (さくら) instead of kanji (桜).

		Family name	Given name
Female	Japanese	山口	珠子
	romanised	Yamaguchi	Tamako
Male	Japanese	中村	広
	romanised	Nakamura	Hiroshi

addressing Japanese people

In English-speaking contexts the Japanese use the appropriate English title followed by their family name in formal situations, as shown below. In informal contexts, just the given name is used. In some cases, this may be abbreviated to a nickname. For example, Hiroshi's friends might address him as 'Hiro'.

	Formal address	Informal address
Female	Ms Yamaguchi	Tamako
Male	Mr Nakamura	Hiroshi

Japanese titles

The Japanese titles listed opposite are placed after the name. The most general title, equivalent to the English Mr or Ms, is –san. This is placed after the family name in formal contexts but, in informal settings, may be placed after the personal name instead. In a business setting, people often use family name followed by a company title, such as president, manager, etc.

Title	Comments
-san	General unisex title for adult men and women, placed *after* the name
-sama	Polite form of -san, used to show respect and deference to someone of high status
-sensei	Respectful title used for teachers, doctors and other authority figures
-chan	Unisex title which means 'little', used for children; it can also be used when speaking to someone much younger or of lower status, or among friends as a term of endearment
-kun	Similar to 'Master': used to address boys or men much younger or lower in status than the speaker

wives and children

In Japan, married couples are legally required to share the same family name. In theory this family name could be either the husband's or the wife's; in practice the wife nearly always changes her family name to her husband's. For example, if the Japanese people in the examples on the previous page were to marry, Yamaguchi Tamako would change her name to Nakamura Tamako. Some educated, professional Japanese women may retain their own family name unofficially at work, but this is less common than it is in English-speaking countries. After divorce, Japanese women typically reclaim their maiden names.

Children take the family name shared by their parents, which is usually the father's family name. Occasionally, children might be given a name containing a kanji from one of their parents' names. For example, Miwa (美和) might give her daughter the name Mio (美央), so that names of both mother and daughter contain the same kanji.

anglicising Japanese names

Although an occasional, high-status traditional Japanese man might refuse to change his name for anyone, the great majority of Japanese people simply swap their names around in English-speaking contexts so that they mimic the given name + surname style of Anglo-Saxon names. The example names given would be changed to Tamako Yamaguchi and Hiroshi Nakamura.

Unlike the Chinese, very few Japanese people adopt a Western name, as Japanese names are generally easy for English speakers to pronounce.

entering Japanese names in a database

When entering Japanese names in a Western database, enter the family name in the 'surname' field and the given name in the 'given name' field. If the Japanese person uses a nickname or short version of his or name (e.g. 'Hiro') this should be placed under 'preferred name'.

	Given name	Surname	Preferred name
Female	Tamako	Yamaguchi	Tamachan
Male	Hiroshi	Nakamura	Hiro

pronunciation

consonants

Most consonants in romanised Japanese are pronounced more or less as they are in English, except those shown below.

Consonant	Pronunciation
f	Pronounced by pushing air between narrowed lips (rather than forcing air between the top teeth and lower lip, as with the English 'f')
n	As in 'nut' at the start of a syllable. Like 'ng' in 'sing' at the end of the syllable, unless followed by a syllable starting with a p or a b, when it is 'm' as in 'mat'
r	Pronounced somewhere between an 'l' and a 'd'

The sounds represented by f and r in romanised Japanese do not exist in English, and are difficult for English speakers to pronounce. If you cannot manage these sounds, simply pronounce these letters as you would in English. Most English speakers will be doing this, and people with Japanese names will probably be used to hearing this in English-speaking contexts.

The variable pronunciation of the letter n in romanised Japanese can be confusing for English speakers. The n written at the end of syllables in Japanese is an unusual kana (Japanese syllabary symbol) represented by ん in hiragana and ン in katakana. The effect of this kana is to nasalise the sound. At the end of most syllables, as in the title '-san', this sounds to an English-speaking ear as though the word ends with an **ng**. However, when a syllable ending with ん or ン is followed by a **b** or a **p**, as in the word 'kanpai', the nasalising effect results in an **m** sound. In such cases, the kana may sometimes be romanised as an **m** to indicate this, hence 'kampai'.

vowels

Japanese has only five vowel sounds, which are pronounced as shown below. These may be pronounced short or long (pronounced the same as short vowels but held for longer).

In the most commonly used version of the Hepburn system, long vowels are marked with a circumflex (ô) or macron (ō) or written as a double vowel (oo). You may also see the vowels e and o lengthened by adding an i (ei) and u (ou) respectively. For example, the double i in **oishii** indicates a long **i** sound; and the **o** in the name of Japan's capital city should actually be written **Tōkyō** or **Tookyoo**. You may even see a long **o** rendered as **ou**, **Toukyou**. However, in practice, the Japanese usually leave off the macrons for long vowels, which is why we are used to seeing it written **Tokyo**.

In the table below, the most commonly used romanisation for long vowels is placed first. *All* syllables in romanised Japanese end in a vowel, an **n** or an **m** (see above).

a	As in 'father'	o	As in 'core'
ā, â, aa	As above, but longer	o, oo, ô, ou	As above, but longer
e	As in 'jet'	u	As in 'put'

ei, ē, ê	As above, but longer	ū, û, uu	As above, but longer
i	Like ee in 'bee'		
ii, ī, î	As above, but longer		

common Japanese family names

Ten of the most common family names in Japan are provided in the following table, with a guide to pronunciation. Note that the syllable 'taw' in this guide should be pronounced in the English way, with rounded lips.

Name	Pronunciation	Name	Pronunciation
Sato	Sah-taw	Ito	Ee-taw
Suzuki	Soo*-zoo-kee	Nakamura	Nah-kah-moo-rah
Takahashi	Tah-kah-ha-shee	Yamamoto	Yah-mah-maw-taw
Tanaka	Tah-nah-kah	Kobayashi	Kaw-bah-yah-shee
Watanabe	Wah-tah-nah-beh	Saito	Sah-ee-taw

*Note that all instances of 'oo' in these examples are pronounced 'oo' as in 'book', not as in 'cool'.

common Japanese given names

Boys tend to receive names which represent virtues, like will, strength and achievement, whereas girls tend to receive names which represent flowers, seasons, generosity and beauty. Second-generation Japanese children living in English-speaking countries are often given English names which can be pronounced in Japanese, such as Ken, Naomi and Mary.

From about the 1940s to the 1960s, the majority of Japanese girls were given names ending in -ko (子), which means 'child'. In the 1960s and 1970s, names ending in -mi (美), which means 'beautiful', also became popular. Since the 1980s, -ko names and to a lesser extent mi names have become increasingly unfashionable, and names with a wide range of other endings, such as -e, -ka, -ra, -yo, -o and -ai are replacing them.

Boys in the mid-20th century were commonly given names consisting of a single kanji, such as Hiroshi (広) and Makoto (誠), and names ending in -ro (郎), which means 'son'. Names based on birth order were common, with the first son being called Ichiro (first son), the second Jiro (second son), the third Saburo (third son) and so on. This practice is now almost obsolete, and names which comprise two kanji and end in -ki, -shi, -ro, -ta and -ya are now popular.

Era	Men	Women
pre-1960	Hiroshi, Isamu, Masaru, Shigeru, Takashi	Kazuko, Keiko, Sachiko, Setsuko, Yōko
1960–80	Daisuke, Kenichi, Makoto, Naoki, Takeshi	Akemi, Junko, Kumiko, Mayumi, Tomomi, Yumiko
1980–90	Daiki, Daisuke, Kenta, Shōta	Ai, Mai, Megumi, Miho, Rie
1990 onwards	Takuya, Tatsuya, Tsubasa	Aimi, Asuka, Misaki, Nanami, Sakura

chapter 8
Vietnamese
names

background

about the Vietnamese language

Like Korean, Vietnamese was originally written using
Chinese characters. In the 10th century, these characters
were adapted for the Vietnamese language into a system
called chữ nôm, which was used until around the 16th
century, when Catholic missionaries from Portugal began
work on a system of romanisation. The man credited
with the development of quốc ngữ, the system still used
today (albeit in modernised form), was a Jesuit priest
called Father Alexandre de Rhodes, who published a
Latin–Vietnamese dictionary in 1651.

Quốc ngữ uses the Roman alphabet, minus the letters
f, j, w and z (f and z are occasionally seen in North
Vietnam, but are not officially part of quốc ngữ), and
with the addition of the seven extra letters đ, ă, â, ê, ô, ơ
and ư. The diacritics on these seven letters modify their
pronunciation from the way the unmarked letters d, a, e,

o and u are pronounced, just as the e in café has been modified with a diacritic called an acute accent.

Vietnamese is a tonal language (see page 28), and many Vietnamese words and names therefore also have diacritics on them to indicate the tone with which they are to be pronounced. The five tone markings used in Vietnamese are shown below.

Word	Meaning	Pitch of voice
ma	ghost	Mid-level and flat
má	mother	High rising
mà	but	Low falling
mả	tomb	Begins low, falls, and then rises gently
mã	horse	Begins mid-level, drops and cuts off, then goes back up (sounds like buh-uh)
mạ	rice seedling	Voice drops and cuts off abruptly

When the marks used to indicate pronunciation are combined with the marks used to indicate tone, the result can be quite complex: ẳ, ư', etc.

about Vietnamese names

Up until a few decades ago, most Vietnamese people had four names, of which the first was the family name, the second was a gender marker (Văn for men or Thị for women), the third was a generation name, and the fourth was a personal name. This has begun to change in the last 20 or 30 years.

The use of Văn as a gender marker is now rare in

Vietnam, though some men may retain it as a middle name. The female gender marker Thị is still in use, though many women now drop it except on very official documents such as their birth certificates. The use of a generation name shared by same-sex siblings is much less common among the Vietnamese than it is among the Chinese. Instead, most Vietnamese simply have a 'middle name' which is not shared by same-sex siblings. Sometimes parents choose names with the same initial for their children instead.

In Vietnam, the parents (or sometimes grandparents) typically choose names for their meaning. Children may be named after desirable virtues, such as courage, kindness or fidelity. Sometimes the middle name and first name will combine to form a phrase, such as Thanh Thuy, 'clear water'.

structure

examples of Vietnamese names

Few Vietnamese men still use Văn as a gender marker, and although maybe 50 per cent of women still have Thị on their birth certificates, marriage certificates and passports, most drop it for other forms of identification.

	Family name	Gender marker	Middle name	Personal name
Female	Trần	Thị	Thanh	Hương
Male	Nguyễn	(Văn)	Đinh	Tuấn

addressing Vietnamese people

Most Vietnamese people use title + family name for formal address in English-speaking contexts. In Vietnamese contexts, however, title + personal name is sometimes seen (see 'Vietnamese titles' below). For informal address, most Vietnamese people use just their personal name, although you may occasionally encounter a Vietnamese woman who prefers to be addressed by middle name + personal name instead, i.e. Thanh Hương.

	Formal address	Informal address
Female	Ms Trần	Hương
Male	Mr Nguyễn	Tuấn

Vietnamese titles

In formal and business contexts, Vietnamese titles are usually placed before the full name or the family name, e.g. Ông Nguyễn. Among family members and in less formal situations, however, title + given name may be used. For example, Trần Thị Thanh Hương's nephew might address her as Cô Hương.

Title	English equivalent	Title	English equivalent
Ông	Mr	Cô	Ms (for young women)
Bà	Ms (for older women)	Bác Sĩ	Dr

wives and children

In Vietnam, women do not change their family name after marriage. However, when living in an English-speaking country, Vietnamese women often follow local custom and use Mrs with their husband's family name.

Children take their father's family name.

anglicising Vietnamese names

The quốc ngữ romanisation system, with its complex diacritics and pronunciation based on Portuguese and French, is difficult for English speakers to use. As a result, Vietnamese people usually adapt their names for English-speaking contexts.

Almost all Vietnamese people remove the diacritics from their names when filling in forms in an English-speaking context. Many also adapt the way their names are pronounced or spelt. One well-known example of this is the very common family name Nguyễn. Although the Vietnamese pronunciation of this name is something like 'ngwee-un', it is frequently pronounced as 'new-yun' or 'na-goy-un' in English-speaking contexts, because these pronunciations are more logical for English speakers. Another example can be seen with the family name Dương, which some southern Vietnamese families change to 'Dzerng' because this spelling gives English speakers a better idea of how they pronounce it.

It is also common for Vietnamese people to adapt their name to fit the Anglo-Saxon given name + surname structure. For example, many Vietnamese people drop their middle name and swap their remaining names around to give 'Huong Tran' and 'Tuan Nguyen'. Others might adopt a Western given name and use it with their family name (e.g. Helen Tran, John Nguyen). Children of Vietnamese background born in an English-speaking country, however, may be given an official Western name as well as, or even instead of, a Vietnamese given name and middle name.

entering Vietnamese names in a database

When entering Vietnamese names into a Western database, enter the family name under 'surname', the personal name under 'given name' and the middle name under 'middle name'. If Thị (or, less likely, Văn) is present, either omit it or include it under 'middle name'. If the person is using a Western name, this should be placed under 'preferred name'. If in doubt, ask the person for clarification.

	Given name	Middle name	Surname	Preferred name
Female	Huong	Thanh	Tran	Huong, Helen
Male	Tuan	Dinh	Nguyen	Tuan, John

pronunciation

initial consonants

There are significant regional variations in Vietnamese pronunciation. The same name may be pronounced differently in North and South Vietnam. This can be confusing for English speakers. Note especially the differences in the way the letters d and tr are described in the table opposite.

c	'c' as in 'cat'	ph	Like 'ph' in 'photo'
d	North Vietnam = 'z' in 'zoo'; South Vietnam = 'y' in 'yes'	q	Similar to the 'w' in 'wax'
đ	'd' as in 'dog'	s	Similar to the 'sh' in 'shut'
g	Like 'y' in 'yak' when followed by 'i', otherwise as in 'girl'	th	Similar to the 't' in 'top'
kh	Gutteral 'k' sound pronounced in the throat; similar to the 'ch' in the Scottish word 'loch'	tr	South Vietnam = like 'tr' in 'trick'; North Vietnam = like the 'dge' in 'edge'
nh	Like the 'ny' in 'canyon'	x	Similar to 's' in 'sock'
ng	Like 'ng' in 'sing', but softer		

vowels and endings

The table on the on the next page comprises letters and longer endings which you may see in Vietnamese names. The pronunciations given in this section are approximations only, as there are many sounds in Vietnamese which have no exact equivalent in English.

a	As in 'father'	ô	Like 'aw' in 'raw'
â	Like 'e' in 'fern', but shorter	oan	'wahn' (similar to the word 'one')
ach	Between 'ark' and 'uk' (with the 'k' almost silent)	oang	like 'wung', to rhyme with 'lung'
ang	'ah' (the 'ng' is almost silent)	uan	'oon' (with 'oo' as in 'book')
anh	'ahn'	uc	'ook' as in 'book' (the 'k' is almost silent)
ao	Like 'ow' as in 'cow'	ui	'oy-ee' ('oy' in 'boy' followed by 'ee' as in 'bee')
e	Like 'a' in 'care'	ung	'oong' ('oo' as in book)
ê	Like 'e' in 'pert'	uong	'erng' (do not pronounce the 'r')
ich	Like 'ik' (with the 'k' almost silent)	uu	'euh-oo' (like 'e' in 'fern' followed by 'oo' in 'pool')
ien	'ee-uhn' (similar to the name 'Ian')	uy	'oo-ee' ('oo' as in 'pool')
iêu	'ee-oh' (like 'eo' in 'Leo')	y	Like 'ee' in 'bee'
uê	Like 'ue' in 'quest'		

common Vietnamese family names

In many cases, Vietnamese people living in an English-speaking country will use an anglicised pronunciation of their names, especially if their names are particularly counter-intuitive for English speakers. For example, Lê is often adapted to sound like 'Lee', **Trần** may be pronounced to rhyme with 'bran', **Đinh** may be adapted to sound like 'Dean', and **Phạm** may be rhymed with 'ham'.

Family name	Pronunciation	Family name	Pronunication
Đặng	Dung (like the English word)	Nguyễn	Ngwee-uhn
Dương	Dzuh-ng (North), Yuh-ng (South)	Phạm	Fum
Khoa	Kwah	Trần	Djun (North), Drun (South)
Lê	Lay	Trường	Druh-ng
Ngo	Ngaw	Vũ	Voo-oo ('oo' as in 'book')

common Vietnamese given names

Because Vietnamese names are particularly difficult for English speakers, lists of common male and female names are provided below with a rough pronunciation guide. Where two syllables are indicated (for example, 'How-ng') run them together as if the name has only one syllable.

Female

Name	Pronunciation	Name	Pronunciation
Anh	Unn	Loan	Law-uhn
Hoa	Hwah	Ngọc*	Ngo' ('o' as in 'pot')
Hồng*	How-ng	Quỳnh	Wn

Female (cont'd)

Name	Pronunciation	Name	Pronunciation
Huê*	Hwe ('e' as in 'jet', but longer)	Thị*	Between 'tay' and 'tee'
Hường	Her-ng (do not pronounce the 'r' in 'her')	Thuý	Tu-wee
Liên	Lee-uhn	Xuân	Soo-un

*Commonly used as a middle name.

Male

Name	Pronunciation	Name	Pronunciation
Cường	Kuh-ng	Nam	Nahm
Đình*	Dn	Phúc	Fook (rhyme with 'book')
Đức	Dook (rhyme with 'book')	Tiến	Dee-uhn
Hùng	Hoong ('oo' as in 'book')	Tuấn	Doo-uhn ('oo' as in 'book')
Linh	Ln	Văn*	Vahn

*Commonly used as a middle name.

chapter 9
Thai
names

background

about the Thai language

There are a number of regional dialects spoken in Thailand, but the official Thai language is the central dialect spoken in and around Bangkok. Thai is a tonal language (see page 28) with five tones. It is written using an abugida (see page 22) developed in the 13th century by King Ramkhamaeng.

Modern Thai contains 44 consonants and 32 vowels. Various romanisation systems have been proposed for the Thai language since the 17th century, but the one most widely used today was developed by the Royal Academic Institute. This system represents sounds phonetically, but does not the incorporate the tones and lengthened vowels used in the Thai language. The limitations of this system (and the fact that less-educated Thai people may not be fully familiar with it) mean that romanised spellings of Thai names and words will not always be a good representation of pronunciation for English speakers. In some cases, several different spellings of the same name or word may be seen.

about Thai names

Thai people have two official names, a given name followed by a surname. Most Thais are also given a short nickname, which they use informally with their friends and family. Thai nicknames often have an odd or comical meaning (such as 'Kai', meaning 'egg', or 'Oun', meaning 'fat') because of an ancient belief that demons prey on children with beautiful names. Although this belief is no longer widely held, most Thai children are still given a nickname shortly after birth.

Selecting the child's official given name is a more serious matter. Traditionally, parents take the child to a Buddhist temple (95 per cent of Thais are Buddhist) and consult a monk, who gives the parents a short list of initials based on the date and time of birth, moon phase and year. After this, either the monk or the parents pick a name starting with an appropriate initial which has a good sound and meaning. More recently, some Thai parents have begun choosing their children's names themselves.

Surnames were added to Thai names around 1913, when King Rama VI, who was educated in England, decreed that Thai people should adopt them. With the exception of a small group of high-status families, who received surnames from the King, Thai people had to come up with their own surname. Many families incorporated Thai words with positive associations (e.g. precious stones, prosperity, blessings) and the names of important ancestors into their surnames.

As the newly selected surnames were registered, families who had chosen the same surname as another family were asked to modify their choice, often by adding further syllables to it. Similarly, immigrants to Thailand who decide to adopt a Thai surname often end up with a name containing a lot of syllables to avoid duplicating an existing name. This is why recent Chinese immigrants to Thailand often have such long surnames.

Thai surnames can be confusing for English speakers because they tend to seem much shorter when they are said aloud than when they appear in written form. This has to do with the fact that Thai surnames are derived from the Sanskrit language. The written form of the name may include many syllables from the original Sanskrit which are not pronounced when the name is used in spoken Thai. When the name is written in Thai, these 'silent' syllables are indicated with diacritics that 'mute' the syllable to which they are added.

structure

examples of Thai names

Thai names have the same given name + surname pattern as Anglo-Saxon names, though Thai names are used differently (see section on 'Thai titles' on page 118).

		Given name	Surname	Nickname
Male	Thai	ธนพันธ์	โชคพิพัฒน์ผล	ต้น
	Romanised	Thanapan	Chokpipatpol	Ton
Female	Thai	จิรารัตย์	พัฒนเจริญ	ไก่
	Romanised	Jirarat	Phathanacharoen	Kai

addressing Thai people

In Thailand, people use title + given name for formal address. However, in English-speaking contexts, Thai people may follow the Anglo-Saxon custom of using title + surname for formal address. Note that in Thailand surnames are seldom used except in administrative contexts.

	Formal address (Thai)	Formal address (Western)	Informal address
Male	Mr Thanapun	Mr Chokpipatpol	Ton
Female	Miss Jirarat	Ms Phathanacharoen	Kai

School teachers in Thailand address children by their given names, but friends, family and even colleagues typically address each other by nickname, except in the most formal settings or when the person being addressed is of very high status. Thai men are somewhat more likely to use formal address than women. If in doubt, it is best to begin by addressing a Thai person formally by title + given name and then wait to be invited to use the nickname.

Thai titles

In Thai, titles are placed before the given name (e.g. Mo Thanapan). The most commonly used title in Thailand is Khun (see table opposite).

Title	Comments
Khun	General purpose unisex title used to indicate politeness
Nai	Used for men aged over 15
Nang	Equivalent of Mrs; used for married women
Nang Sao	Equivalent of Miss; used for unmarried women over 15
Mo	Equivalent of Doctor
Kroo	Used for teachers

wives and children

Until 2004, Thai wives were obliged by the Names Act to replace their surname with their husband's surname upon marriage. This Act has now been revoked, and Thai women can choose to retain their maiden name, or to use their maiden name and add their husband's surname onto the end, though it may be some years before this is common practice. Remember that Thais use title + given name, not surname, for formal address; hence, if Ton and Kai married, Kai's name would change to Jirarat Chokpipatpol, but she would be addressed as Mrs Jirarat.

Children inherit their father's surname, unless their parents have decided to use the mother's surname or they are born of an unmarried mother.

anglicising Thai names

Some Thais anglicise their names to 'nickname + given name' in English-speaking contexts (e.g. Ton Thanapan, Kai Jirarat). This encourages English speakers to address them in the correct Thai manner, with nickname for informal address and 'title + given name' for formal address. This works well for everyday use but can cause confusion with databases.

entering Thai names in a database

When entering Thai names in a Western database, place the Thai given name in the 'given name' field, the surname in the 'surname' field, and place the nickname in the 'preferred name' field. Note that databases should be designed to accommodate names of at least 20 letters to ensure that Thai surnames (many of which have 15 letters or more) can be entered in full. If your database does not allow enough space, you may need to shorten the name, usually to as much as can be fitted in. If possible, let the Thai person know about this problem and warn him or her about the name shortening.

Although Thai people use their nickname like an English given name, it is best to enter it under 'preferred name'. This is because the nickname is not actually part of the person's official name. If your database does not have a 'preferred name' field, it could be added in brackets after the given name instead, for example 'Thanapun (Ton)'.

Title	Given name	Surname	Preferred name
Mr	Thanapun	Chokpipatpol	Ton
Ms	Jirarat	Phathanacharoen	Kai

pronunciation

consonants

Romanised Thai does not contain **q**, **x** or **z**. If a consonant is not listed below, it is pronounced in the same way as in English. Note that in Thai most final consonants are not pronounced. For example, the **p** on the end of 'thip' is not pronounced. Instead, the sound stops abruptly after the **i**, in what is called a glottal stop.

k	Unaspirated 'k' as in 'skin'	t	Unaspirated 't' as in 'stop'
kh	As in 'kite'	th	Aspirated 't' as in 'top'
ng	Like the 'ng' in 'sing'	r	Slightly rolled, as in the Spanish 'r'
p	Unaspirated 'p' as in 'spin'	v, w	Both pronounced like the 'w' in 'wash'
pb	Aspirated 'b' as in 'bag'	ph	Like the 'p' in 'pin"

vowels

a	Like 'u' in 'cup'	ao	Like the 'ow' in 'cow'
aa	Like 'a' in 'father'	e	As in 'jet'
ae	Like 'a' in 'cat'	eh	As above, but longer
ai	As in 'aisle'	eu	Like the 'u' in 'fur' (mouth more rounded and closed than the 'e' in 'fern')

eua	Like the 'u' in 'fur' followed by the 'a' in 'father'	oe	Like the 'e' in 'fern'
i	As in 'tin'	u	Like the 'u' in 'flute'
ia	As in 'Mia'	ua	Like the 'ou' in 'tour'
iaw	Like 'eo' in 'Leo'	uay	Like 'oo' in 'pool' plus 'ai' in 'aisle'
o	Like the 'o' in 'go'		

common Thai surnames

Because every family in Thailand was asked to come up with a unique surname, Thai people who share the same surname will always be related. The most common surnames in Thailand are therefore the surnames of people who have the largest families! Rather than list the largest families in Thailand, this section provides a list of syllables commonly found in Thai surnames. Note that a **p** which is not followed by an **h** (as in the pronunciation guide) is *unaspirated*, and may sound a bit more like a **b** to an English speaker.

Syllable (meaning)	Approximate pronunciation	Syllable (meaning)	Approximate pronunciation
charoen (prosperity)	chah-reuhn	phan (unity)	Like the word 'pun'
jira (sacred)	jee-rah	pol (power)	poll
korn (hand of God)	Like 'corn' (Aus/NZ/UK), 'kawn' (US/Can)	pon (yield)	pon

Syllable (meaning)	Approximate pronunciation	Syllable (meaning)	Approximate pronunciation
nara (good)	nah-rah	pong (increasing)	pong
ngam (beautiful)	ngahm	porn (blessing)	pawn
pat (holy)	paht	rat (scripture of Buddha)	raht

common Thai given names

In Thai, male names often end in **-chai**, **-korn**, **-phan**, **-pol** and **-sak**; female names often end in **-a**, **-ee** and **-thip**.

Male	Charoensak, Chattiphan, Chokchai, Nakorn, Nikorn, Peerapan, Peerapat, Ronnachai, Sookaphan, Somchai
Female	Aranee, Jiraporn, Jirarat, Maleega, Maleewan, Panna, Pataree, Pornthip, Puangthip, Sunisa, Suwanna, Suwanee

common Thai nicknames

Thai nicknames can be the names of animals, everyday objects, fruits (for girls) and sounds. Short English names such as 'Nick' or 'Tom' are also becoming popular as nicknames.

success with Asian names

Male	Boon, Ne, Nong, Ott, Pon, Sing, Suea, Ton
Female	Gib, Jam, Jig, Kai, Manao, Ning, Pam, Pong, Porn, Som, Wan
Unisex	Gai, Gob, Mu, Nok, Nui, Pbla

chapter 10
Khmer
names

background

about the Khmer language

The official language of Cambodia is *Khmer*, which is derived from the language of the Angkor Empire which once encompassed much of South-East Asia. Khmer is spoken by about 90 per cent of the population of Cambodia and written using an abugida (page 22) derived from the *Brahmi* script of ancient India. Unlike the national languages of neighbouring Thailand and Vietnam, Khmer is a non-tonal language.

Most Cambodians romanise their names based on a system developed by the French during the colonial period. This system uses diacritics (accents) to modify the sounds of roman letters to accommodate sounds in Khmer which are not present in French. For example, the letter **a** is used for the sound **ah**, and an **a** with a circumflex on it (**â**) is used for the sound **ow** (as in 'how'). The French also used the letter **r** to lengthen vowel sounds. For example, the o in **chon** is pronounced as in 'pot', whereas the o in **chorn** is the same sound but held for twice as long.

As the correct use of this system is not widely known among Cambodians, it is common to see a number of spellings of the same names and words. Note that Cambodian people usually leave out the diacritics in their names when staying in an English-speaking country.

There is now another system, developed by the Congress Library in the United States, which is used only for official documents in written Khmer. This is a transliteration system, in which every Khmer symbol has a direct Roman equivalent. This may be used to romanise names on very formal documents, but is very rarely seen in everyday life.

about Khmer names

India and China have both played a part in shaping Khmer names. Many centuries ago, the Khmer nobility used Sanskrit names, and even today many popular given names show a Sanskrit influence. Since the Angkor period, there has also been a strong influence from China: 30 to 40 per cent of modern Cambodians have some Chinese ancestry, and some of these people now follow the Chinese naming system with a family name, generation name and personal name.

Before the 20th century, ordinary Cambodians had only a given name. During the French colonial period, however, French administrators pressured people to adopt family names so that they could be registered. Many Cambodians decided to use the given name of their father or grandfather as a family name. These new family names were placed before the given names, following the Chinese pattern.

Cambodian names are traditionally selected in consultation with a Buddhist monk, who informs the family about which initials and names would be most auspicious for the child. This practice is now becoming less common, with more and more families preferring to select children's names themselves. Names are chosen for their sound and meaning, with more educated parents placing much emphasis on the latter.

Note that you may also encounter people with Khmer names from Thailand and Vietnam.

structure

examples of Khmer names

Most older Cambodians have two names, but among the young and for those with Chinese ancestry, three names are often seen. About 60 per cent of Khmers also have nicknames, which are given when the child is born. These are often shortenings of the given name, or terms linked to appearance and birth order which mean 'little girl', 'little boy', 'big one', etc.

		Family name	Middle name	Given name	Nickname
Male	Khmer	នួន		សំណាង	ជ្រូក
	romanised	Noun		Samnang	Chrouch
Female	Khmer	សាយ	សុខ	សុភី	ធូច
	romanised	Say	Sok	Sophy	Touch

addressing Khmer people

In formal correspondence, Cambodian names should be written out in full; otherwise, title + family name is usual. Informally, Cambodians may use either their given name, a shortened form of their given name, or the short nickname given to them during childhood.

	Formal address (spoken)	Formal address (written)	Informal address
Female	Mr Noun	Mr Noun Samnang	Samnang, Chrouch
Male	Ms Say	Ms Say Sok Sophy	Sophy, Phy, Touch

Khmer titles

Khmer titles are placed before the given name alone (Lork Noun, Neak Srey Say) in informal situations, and placed before the full name in writing and formal situations. **Lork** and **Neak Srey** (casually abbreviated to **Neak**) may also be used on their own in a similar way to 'Sir' and 'Madam' in English.

Title	Comments
Lork	Equivalent of Mr
Lork Srey	Similar to Madam: a general title for high-ranking women
Neak Srey	Equivalent of Mrs, used for married women

| Kanha | Equivalent of Miss, for young, unmarried women |
| Neang | General title for women, similar to Ms |

wives and children

Cambodian women do not change their names after marriage. However, in Cambodia they may sometimes be addressed as **Neak Srey** followed by their husband's full name (Neak Sray Noun Samnang). In English-speaking contexts, some may follow Anglo-Saxon tradition and use Mrs + husband's family name, or change their official family name to their husband's (Noun Sok Sophy).

Chinese Cambodian children usually take their father's family name; ethnic Cambodians may take their father's given name as a family name instead.

anglicising Khmer names

Most Cambodians anglicise their names by placing their given name first and their family name last (e.g. Samnang Noun). If a middle name is present, this is usually dropped. For example, Say Sok Sophy would probably change her name to Sophy Say.

entering Khmer names in a database

When entering Khmer names in a database, place the given name under 'given name', the middle name (if present) under 'middle name', and the family name under 'surname'. If the Khmer person regularly uses a nickname or shortened version of his or her name, place this under 'preferred name'. If your database does not have a 'preferred name' field, the nickname can be placed after the given name in brackets, for example 'Sophy (Touch)'.

	Given name	Middle name	Surname	Preferred name
Female	Samnang		Noun	Chrouch
Male	Sophy	Sok	Say	Touch

pronunciation

consonants

If a consonant is not listed below, it is pronounced in the same way as in English.

ch*	Like the 'dge' in 'edge'	ph	Like the 'p' in 'pin'
chh	Like the 'tch' in 'itch'	pk	Like the 'pk' in 'pipkin'
gn	Like the 'ng' in 'sing'	ps	Like the 'ps' in 'lips'
ks	Like the 'ks' in 'yaks'	t	Like the aspirated 't' in 'top'
nh	Like the 'ny' in 'canyon'	th	Like the unaspirated 't' in 'stop'
p	Like the 'p' in 'spin'		

*Consonants falling on the end of names are clipped very short. For example, when 'uch' falls on the end of a name, as in the common nickname 'Tauch', it is pronounced like a very short 'ee' sound, i.e. 'Taw-ee'.

vowels

a	As in 'father'	o	Either as in 'toe' or as in 'core'
â	Like the 'aw' in 'raw'	oe	Like 'u' in 'blur' (similar to above, but with mouth more closed and rounded)
e	As in 'jet', but longer	oeu	Like 'ee' in 'bee' plus 'u' in 'blur'
eu	Like 'e' in 'fern'	u	As in 'put'
i	Either like 'e' in 'jet' or like 'ee' in 'bee'		

common Khmer family names

The following family names are common among Cambodians.

Name	Approximate pronunciation	Name	Approximate pronunciation
Chea	chee-uh	Say	sah-ee
Kong	koo-ong (oo as in 'book')	Sin	sin
Nheuk	nyeu (pronounce eu like 'e' in 'fern')	So	Like the word 'so'
Noun	noo-un (oo as in 'book')	Sor	saw
Prak	p-ruh	Tan	tahn
Ros	roo-uh	Ung	eung (e in 'fern' plus ng in 'sing')

common Khmer given names

The stress in most Khmer names is placed on the last syllable of the name. In the examples below, the stressed syllable is indicated by **bold type**.

female

Name	Approximate pronunciation	Name	Approximate pronunciation
Bopha	baw-**pa**	Phally	paw-**lee**
Chantha	jahn-**ta**	Sokha	saw-**ka**
Kunthea	koon-**tee**-ah	Sophy	saw-**pee**
Neari	nee-ree	Sophoan	saw-**pwahn**

male

Name	Approximate pronunciation	Name	Approximate pronunciation
Chamroen	jum-**reun**	Sitha	see-**ta**
Dara	da-**ra**	Sombat	som-**ba**
Rithty	ruh-**tee**	Veasna	viz-**nah**
Samnang	sahm-**nahng**	Vuth	voot ('oo' as in 'book')

common Khmer nicknames

Nicknames most often refer to a person's place in the family, that is, where they are in the birth order with respect to their siblings.

birth order names

Name (meaning)	Approximate pronunciation
Srey Tauch (girl)	sry (to rhyme with 'sky') toh-i (like 'toey', except clipped short)
Srey Touch (little girl)	sry too-ee
Srey Thom (older girl)	sry tom
Srey Aun (little sister)	sry oh-un
Srey Borng (elder sister)	sry bawng
Srey Poeuv (littlest sister)	sry poe-er
Mouy (little sister)	mwee
Pros (boy)	praw
Pros Touch (little boy)	praw too-ee
Pros Thom (older boy)	praw tom
Tri (little brother)	tuh-ree

other nicknames

Name (meaning)	Approximate pronunciation
Chrouch (pickle)	ch-rock
Pech (diamond)	Like 'pe' in 'pet'
Siey Leak (Virtuous girl)	sry lee-uh

chapter 11
Hindi
names

general background on Indian names

India has great religious and linguistic diversity. Although
82 per cent of Indians are Hindus, there is also a large
minority of Muslims (12 per cent) and a number of
smaller religious groups, including Christians, Sikhs,
Buddhists and Jains. The national languages of India
are Hindi and English; each state within India also has
its own state language, bringing the number of officially
recognised languages to a total of 18.

Indian naming customs are intrinsically linked to
both religion and language. Hindus typically give their
children the names of gods and goddesses, and names
taken from sacred texts; Muslims often give their
children one of the many names of Allah and the Prophet
Muhammed or his companions and descendants; and
the smaller religious groups have their own naming
traditions. There is also a significant divide between
the names from the north of India, which belong to
the Indo-Aryan language family, and those from the

south, which belong to the Dravidian language family. Each individual language has its own patterns, but as a general rule, names become longer from north to south, and the northerners tend to approximate the Anglo-Saxon given name + surname structure, whereas the southerners more often apply the older tradition of placing the father's name before the given name, rather than including a surname.

This great diversity makes it difficult to refer to 'Indian names' in any meaningful way. I chose to cover *Hindi* as my representative northern Indian language because it is the official language of the Indian government and one of the national languages of India. The naming customs among Hindu speakers of Hindi can, to some degree, be generalised to Hindus who speak other northern languages closely related to Hindi, such as *Gujarati* and *Marathi*, though the spelling of the actual names will vary somewhat between languages.

Tamil, chapter 13, was chosen as a representative of the Dravidian languages because although there are more speakers of *Telugu*, Tamils have a very large world-wide diaspora.

The names of the Sikhs, chapter 12, were selected for a similar reason: although Sikhs comprise only 2 per cent of the population of India, there is a large Sikh diaspora, with many Sikhs living in Western countries.

Two other languages from the Indian subcontinent are covered, namely *Urdu*, chapter 15, and *Bangla*, chapter 16. Urdu is the official language of Pakistan, but is also spoken by several million people in India. Bangla, the official language of Bangladesh, is more or less the same language as *Bengali*, the official language of the Indian state of West Bengal. There are some differences between Indian and Pakistani Urdu names, and between Indian and Bangladeshi Bengali names, but these chapters still provide a good basic overview of names from these languages.

background on Hindi names

about the Hindi language

Hindi is an Indo-European language derived from Sanskrit, which is spoken in north and central India. Hindi is spoken by about 20 per cent of Indians as a mother tongue, and by millions more as a second language. The Indian government originally intended to make Hindi the official national language of India after the country gained independence in 1947, but this plan was abandoned due to protest from southern Indians, who argued that this policy would disadvantage speakers of southern languages from the Dravidian family. These protests were addressed by making the national languages English and Hindi, and allowing each state to nominate its own official state language.

The script, grammar and spelling of Hindi was standardised by the Indian government in the 1950s. Hindi is written in a script called *Devanāgarī* which is also used to write Marathi, *Nepali*, *Prakrit* and Sanskrit. Devanāgarī is an abugida (see page 22), and is characterised by a horizontal line on top from which symbols are 'hung'.

There is no official romanisation system for Hindi, but the most commonly used system is the one developed by the National Library of Calcutta. This system lengthens vowels by placing a macron over them (e.g. ā) and indicates aspirated consonants (see page 60) by inserting an h after the standard consonant. For example, the k in 'Kiran' would be pronounced like the gentler k in 'skin', whereas the kh in 'Khushal' would be pronounced like the k in 'kin', which has a sharper accompanying exhalation of air.

about Hindi names

Naming customs are similar for Hindus who speak Hindi and other related northern Indian languages. Names are chosen for their meaning as well as their sound, usually by a child's parents. Sometimes parents may choose a name starting with one of the initials designated for the day of the lunar month on which the child was born, or consult an astrologer to help identify an auspicious name; sometimes they simply choose the name themselves from a book or other source.

Given names are often derived from the names of gods and goddesses, or drawn from the holy text of the god particularly revered by the child's family. Other possible name sources include characters from literature, personal virtues such as compassion or wisdom, famous people and the names of trees and flowers.

Most Hindi speakers have a given name and a surname. The surname indicates the caste or subcaste to which a person belongs. There are four castes, with the highest being the *Brahmin* or priest caste, followed by the *Kshatriya* or warrior caste, the *Vaishya* or merchant caste, and the *Sudra* or servant caste.

structure

examples of Hindi names

Hindi names are structured in the same way as Anglo-Saxon names.

		Given name	Surname
Male	Devanāgarī	राहुल	शर्मा
	romanised	Rahul	Sharma
Female	Devanāgarī	दिव्या	अरोड़ा
	romanised	Divya	Arora

addressing Hindi people

As with Anglo-Saxon names, Hindi speakers should be addressed by title + family name in formal situations and given name in informal situations.

	Formal address	Informal address
Male	Mr Sharma	Rahul
Female	Ms Arora	Divya

Hindi titles

The Hindi titles for Mr and Mrs may be pronounced and spelt in either of the two ways shown opposite.

Title	Comments
Shri, Sri	Mr, placed before the surname, e.g. Shri Sharma
Shrimati	Mrs, placed before the surname, e.g. Shrimati Arora
Kumari	Miss, placed before the given name, e.g. Kumari Divya, now rarely used
-ji	Placed on the end of a name to show respect, e.g. Divyaji; may be used with the given name or surname, depending on the situation

wives and children

Women usually change their surname to their husband's after marriage, although a growing minority may add it onto the end of their existing name instead (and an occasional professional woman might keep her maiden name). For example, if Rahul and Divya were to marry, Divya would probably change her name to Divya Sharma, or possibly Divya Arora Sharma. However, as 'Sharma' is a Brahmin surname and 'Arora' is a Kshatriya surname, they would be unlikely to marry: Hindus usually marry within their own caste.

Children inherit their father's surname.

anglicising Hindi names

North Indian Hindi names follow the Anglo-Saxon structure and thus do not need to be anglicised. Note that Hindus are very unlikely to adopt English names (as may be seen among Buddhists and Confucians): these are seen as Christian. Note, however, that Indians and

Anglo-Indians who are Christian often have completely Western names (e.g. Lisa Matthew).

entering Hindi names in a database

As most Hindi names follow the same basic structure as Anglo-Saxon names, they can be entered in a database in the same way as an English name, with the given name under 'given name' and the surname under 'surname'. If the person uses a nickname, as many Indians do, this can be placed under 'preferred name'.

	Given name	Middle name	Surname	Preferred name
Male	Rahul		Sharma	
Female	Divya		Arora	Div

pronunciation

consonants

ch	As in 'chip'	sh	As in 'ship'
g	As in 'girl'	t	Unaspirated 't', as in 'stop'
d	Pronounced with the tongue curled behind the front teeth	th	Aspirated 't', as in 'tin'
kh	Like 'ch' in 'loch'	v,w	May both be pronounced somewhere between a 'w' and 'v'
r	Slightly rolled, as in Spanish 'r'		

vowels

a	Like 'u' in 'bun'	ee, ī	As in 'bee'
aa or ā	Like 'a' in 'father'	i	As in 'tin'
ai	Like 'a' in 'care' before a consonant, as in 'aisle' at the end of a word	o	Like 'aw' in 'raw'
au	Like 'aw' in 'raw'	oo, ū	As in 'pool'
e	As in 'they'	u	As in 'put'

common Hindi family names

Indian Hindus can usually determine the caste to which a person belongs by looking at their surname. For example, they would know that a person with the surname Bhat would probably be of the Brahmin caste, whereas a Thakur would be of Kshatriya caste and Gupta would be of Vaishya caste. Rajput and Kumar are sometime adopted as surnames by people from lower castes to disguise their origins.

Name	Pronunciation	Name	Pronunciation
Arora	ah-raw-rah	Rai	Like the word 'rye'
Bhat	baht	Rajput	razh-put
Kumar	koo-mar ('oo' as in 'book')	Reddy	Like the word 'ready'
Mathur	mah-tour	Sharma	shah-ruh-ma
Patel	pah-tell	Thakur	tah-koor ('oo' as in 'book')
Pillai	pee-lye	Yadav	yah-dahv

common Hindi given names

In the examples below, 'younger generation' refers to people born around the 1970s or later. This division is not absolute. For example a man called Ashok could be born in the 1980s, but it is more likely that he was born earlier.

	Men	Women
Older generation	Arun, Ashok, Pramod, Rajiv, Ravi, Rohan, Sanjay, Vijay, Vikram	Gita, Hema, Manju, Meena, Meera/Mira, Parvati, Prabha, Radha, Rani, Sita
Younger generation	Abhishek, Ajay, Amit, Pawan, Rahul, Ravi, Rohan, Samir, Sanjay, Vikram	Alka, Amrita, Anita, Anu, Bhavna, Garima, Jyoti, Kiran, Suman

chapter 12
Sikh
names

background

about Sikhism and the Punjabi language

The Sikh religion was founded by Guru Nanak in the 15th century during the period of social unrest under the rule of the Mughuls. Sikhs believe in reincarnation, like Hindus, but their religion is monotheistic and rejects the notion of caste.

There are five traditional symbols to which Sikhs are supposed to adhere. One is the hair or 'kesh', which symbolises godliness and should not be cut. Sikh men traditionally wrap their hair in a turban as it grows. Sikhs are meant to carry a knife called the 'kirpan', representing valour and willingness to defend the faith, and a wooden comb called the 'kangha', a symbol of cleanliness. They should also wear a steel bangle called the 'karha', signifying commitment to the faith, and special cotton underwear called the 'keshera', representing purity. Some modern-day Sikhs are beginning to abandon these symbols, especially in India, though in some expatriate communities these traditions are still strong.

Sikhism developed in the Punjab region, which was divided between India and the newly formed state of Pakistan in 1947. The language spoken in this region is an Indo-European language called *Punjabi*. Punjabi is a tonal language (see page 28) with three tones. In the Indian state of Punjab, it is written in a script called *Gurmukhi*, which means 'from the mouth of the guru'. Gurmukhi is an abugida (see page 22) devised by the Guru Nanak and further developed by the Guru Angad in the 16th century. It contains 35 distinct symbols and nine vowel modifiers. Like Hindi, it is written left to right, and the symbols hang from the line rather than resting on it. In the Pakistani province of Punjab, Punjabi is written in the right-to-left *Shahmukhi* script, a modified form of the *Nastaliq* script used to write Urdu (see page 170).

There is no formal romanisation system specifically designed for Punjabi, though the system developed in the National Library of Calcutta used for most Indian languages is often applied. In this system, vowels are lengthened by adding a macron (e.g. ā).

about Sikh names

In 1699, the 10th guru of the Sikhs, Guru Gobind Singh, ordained that Sikhs drop their Hindu surnames which indicated the subcaste to which their family belonged. Instead, all Sikh men were to adopt the surname **Singh**, meaning 'lion', and all women were to adopt the surname **Kaur**, which means 'princess'.

In the last century or so, due to the difficulties of registration for a people with only two surnames and the demands of the computer era, a growing number of Sikhs are now attaching a family name after the Singh or Kaur. This may be the original caste name, the name of their ancestral village, or even a word related to their appearance (e.g. Dhiddal, meaning 'pot-bellied'). Occasionally you may even encounter a Sikh who omits the Sikh or Kaur for everyday use, leaving only the given name and surname.

Most Sikh given names are ultimately of Sanskrit origin, though you may occasionally see names taken from *Farsi* or English.

Given names are chosen after the child is born. Traditionally, the baby is taken to the temple shortly after birth and brought into the presence of the *Guru Granth Sahib*, which is the sacred text of the Sikhs and regarded as a living guru. The priest opens the *Granth* at a random page and reads an extract called a Shabad. The first letter of the Shabad is chosen as the child's initial. Parents of the child then decide on a name which begins with that initial, often with further input from family and friends.

structure

examples of Sikh names

As detailed above, Sikh women have the religious name Kaur, and Sikh men have the religious name Singh. Most Sikh given names are unisex. Note that very traditional Sikhs omit the surname.

		Given name	Religious name	Surname
Female	Gurmukhi	ਬਲਦੀਪ	ਕੌਰ	ਗਿੱਲ
	romanised	Baldeep	Kaur	Gill
Male	Gurmukhi	ਗੁਰਿੰਦਰ	ਸਿੰਘ	ਸਿੱਧੂ
	romanised	Gurinder	Singh	Sidhu

addressing Sikh people

If Sikhs have a surname after the Singh or Kaur, they should be addressed by title + surname, as shown below. If no surname is present, they should be addressed by title + Singh for men and title + Kaur for women.

For informal address, some Sikhs may use a nickname, or a short form of their name (e.g. 'Bal').

	Formal address	Informal address
Female	Ms Gill	Baldeep
Male	Mr Sidhu	Gurinder

Sikh titles

Titles are rarely used among the Sikhs. The Punjabi title **Sardar** comes from an old word meaning 'army chieftain'. A **-ji** may be placed on the end of a title to make it extra polite and respectful (Sardarji Gurinder). **Sardarji** and **Sardaniji** can also be used on their own for polite address, rather like 'Sir' and 'Madam'.

Title	English equivalent
Sardar	Mr, used with the given name, e.g. Sardar Gurinder
Sardani	Ms, used with the given name, e.g. Sardani Baldeep

wives and children

When women marry, they replace their family name with their husband's. For example, if the two people in the examples above were to marry, Baldeep would change her name to Baldeep Kaur Sidhu. If there is no surname, women simply change their title to Mrs and are addressed as 'Mrs Kaur'. Sikh women may also sometimes be addressed as 'Mrs' followed by their husband's given name (e.g. Mrs Gurinder), especially if there is no surname, as this enables them to distinguish themselves from the millions of other people called Mrs Kaur.

Sons are given the religious name Singh and daughters are given the religious name Kaur. The father's family name, if he uses one, is placed after the religious name.

anglicising Sikh names

When Sikhs are living in English-speaking countries, the use of Singh and Kaur without any further surname to distinguish between families causes a lot of confusion. As a result, many Sikh immigrants adopt a unique surname for administrative reasons. If they prefer not to do this, another possibility is making the name Singh a surname for all family members, adding it after the Kaur on the end of female family members' names (Jasminder Kaur Singh).

entering Sikh names in a database

If a surname is present, enter the Sikh name just as you would an Anglo-Saxon name, placing Singh or Kaur under 'middle name'. If not, enter Singh or Kaur under 'surname'.

	Given name	Middle name	Surname	Preferred name
Female	Baldeep	Kaur	Gill	Baldeep
Male	Gurinder	Singh	Sidhu	Gurinder

common Sikh surnames

Remember that the apparent 'surnames' of many Sikhs will be their religious name, Singh for men and Kaur for women. Among Sikhs who do include surnames with their names, the following are common.

Common Sikh surnames	Arora, Barar, Dhillon, Gill, Grewal, Jandu, Mann, Matharoo, Passi, Randhawa, Sandhu, Sidhu

common Sikh given names

Sikh given names are almost all unisex and often end in **-deep, -inder, -jit/-jeet** (**jit** is more often used for men and **jeet** is more often used for women), **-preet** or **vir/-veer** (**vir** is used for men and **veer** for women).

Common Sikh given names	Amandeep, Amarinder, Baldeep, Baljeet, Daljit, Gurdeep, Harpreet, Jagjivan, Jagvir, Joginder, Karamjeet, Kuldeep, Manjit, Mohinder, Parvir, Ravinder, Satbir, Simranpreet, Sukhveer, Surinder

chapter 13
Tamil
names

background

about the Tamil language

Tamil is from the Dravidian language family and is derived from Sanskrit. It is the official language of the state of Tamil Nadu, and is also widely spoken outside India, due to the large Tamil diaspora. It is spoken as a first language by 18 per cent of the population in Sri Lanka, and is also the most commonly spoken language in the Indian communities of Fiji, Malaysia and Singapore.

Tamil is written using its own script, also called *Tamil*, which is an abugida (see page 22) with 12 basic vowels and 18 basic consonants. These 30 symbols are combined and modified to form 246 different symbols, plus one special character, bringing the total number of symbols in Tamil to 247. The symbols are mostly round and curly in shape, and it is believed that this is because the people originally wrote on palm leaves, on which it was easier to carve curved lines rather than straight ones which might split the leaf.

There is no standard romanisation system for the Tamil language.

about Tamil names

Tamils believe that it is as important for a name to have a positive meaning as it is for it to sound melodious. Their names are often very long, and may contain over 10 letters and more than three syllables. In recent years, however, there has been a trend towards choosing shorter given names, some of northern India origin. This trend may be related to the influence of Bollywood.

After a child is born, Hindu Tamil parents typically consult a priest who will use numerology and astrology to determine an appropriate initial. The parents then choose a name beginning with that initial—often the name of one of the many Hindu gods and goddesses, or a name taken from literature or from the holy text for the god particularly revered by the family.

Although most Tamils are Hindus, there is a strong minority of Christians among Tamils living outside India. Christian Tamils typically choose two given names for their children, one from the Bible and one Tamil name, which they may select in consultation with a respected Christian scholar or senior member of their church.

Most Hindu Tamils do not have surnames. The father's given name is incorporated into the name instead, where it may be either shortened to an initial and placed before the given name (e.g. S. Radhika), or placed after the given name and preceded by either **s/o** (son of) or **d/o** (daughter of), for example Radhika d/o Shanmugam. In the former pattern, other initials may also be present, which could stand for the grandfather's name or the name of the ancestral village.

structure

examples of Tamil names

Hindu Tamil names

If the initial letter of the ancestral village is included in a Tamil name, that letter will be placed first, followed by the initials of male forebears in descending order of age. That is, the great-grandfather's initial would be followed by the grandfather's initial and then by the father's initial, which always precedes the given name.

The examples given below could also be written using the **s/o** (son of) or **d/o** (daughter of) format, i.e. Radhika d/o Shanmugam, and Manavalan s/o Devenapathy. The **s/o** and **d/o** are sometimes dropped, especially among Tamil speakers living in Sri Lanka or in English-speaking countries.

		Father's initial	Other initials	Given name
Female	Tamil	எஸ். (ஷண்முகம்)		ராதிகா
	romanised	S. (Shanmugam)		Radhika
Male	Tamil	டி. (தேவசேனாபதி)	கெ. (குனநாயகம்)	மணவாளன்
	romanised	D. (Devenapathy)	K. (Kunanayagam)	Manavalan

Christian Tamil names

The names of Christian Tamils typically contain a biblical name followed by a Tamil given name, as illustrated below.

		Given name	Second given name	Surname
Female	Tamil	எஸ்தர்	மஞ்ஜுளா	ரத்தினஸிங்கம்
	romanised	Esther	Manjula	Ratnasingham
Male	Tamil	ஜெயிம்ஸ்	அரிரத்தினம்	பிரேமராஜா
	romanised	James	Ariratnam	Premarajah

addressing Tamil people

Tamils commonly use nicknames and short forms for informal address. For example, Manavalan might like to be called 'Manu'.

In India, Hindu Tamils are usually addressed by title + given name (e.g. Mr Manavalan, Miss Radhika). In English-speaking contexts, however, Hindu Tamils commonly anglicise their names by placing their father's given name on the end, which leads English speakers to address them by title + father's given name (e.g. Mr Devenapathy and Ms Shanmugam).

Among Christian Tamils, people use title + surname in formal situations. For informal address, Christian Tamils may use whichever they prefer of their two given names.

	Formal address	**Informal address**
Female Hindu	Ms Shanmugam*	Radhika
Male Hindu	Mr Devenapathy* or Mr Manavalan	Manavalan
Female Christian	Ms Ratnasingham	Esther or Manjula
Male Christian	Mr Premarajah	James or Ariratnam

* Used in English-speaking contexts only.

Tamil titles

There are two different terms in Tamil for each of the standard titles, which can be used interchangeably, although **Shri** and **Shrimathi** are more formal. For Hindus, titles are placed before the given name (Kumari Radhika); for Christians these are placed before the surname (Shri Premarajah).

Title	**English equivalent**	**Title**	**English equivalent**
Shri, Thiru	Mr	Kumar, Kumaran	Master
Shrimathi, Thirumathi	Mrs	Kumari, Selvi	Miss

wives and children

Hindu Tamil

After marriage, Hindu Tamil women drop their father's name and replace it with their husband's given name.

For example, if Manavalan and Radhika were to marry, Radhika would probably change her name to either Radhika Manavalan (dropping the **d/o**) or, much less often, 'Manavalan Radhika' or 'M. Radhika'.

The names of both sons and daughters include their father's given name. This may be placed before the given name, where it is usually abbreviated to an initial, or in full after the given name, where it may be preceded by **s/o** or **d/o**.

Christian Tamil

Among Christian Tamils, women drop their father's surname when they marry and adopt their husband's surname instead. For example, if the people used as examples of Christian Tamil names were to marry, Esther would change her name to Esther Manjula Premarajah.

Children take their father's surname.

anglicising Tamil names

For Hindu Tamils, some part of the name needs to be nominated as a surname in English-speaking contexts. There are two possibilities, either of which may be used. The first is moving the father's given name to the end of the name and using it as a surname, which is effectively using the 'Radhika d/o Shanmugam' or 'Manavalan s/o Devenapathy' structure with the **d/o** and **s/o** dropped out. Unmarried women typically anglicise their names in this way, though they may at first find it strange to be addressed as 'Ms Shanmugam'.

Method 1: Father's name as surname

Original structure	Given name	Patronymic	Father's name
	Radhika	d/o	Shanmugam
Adapted structure	**Given name**	**Surname**	
	Radhika	Shanmugam	

Method 1 is used mostly by women. Men are less inclined to anglicise their names in this way because it means they will be addressed as 'Mr Devenapathy', which is their father's name. Instead, they often use their given name as a 'surname', with their father's name becoming a 'given name', as shown in method 2. This means they will be addressed correctly according to Tamil customs by title + their given name (Mr Manavalan), but it also means that English speakers may ask them why they want to be addressed by their 'surname'.

Method 2: Given name as surname

Original structure	Father's initial	Given name
	D. (initial of Devenapathy)	Manavalan
Adapted structure	**Given name**	**Surname**
	Devenapathy	Manavalan

Christian Tamil

Christian Tamil names do not need to be adapted for English-speaking contexts because they already follow Anglo-Saxon structure.

entering Tamil names in a database

Hindu Tamil names

Hindu Tamil names are particularly difficult to enter into Western databases, due to the absence of a surname, gender differences in structure and the ordering of the components. Unfortunately, there is no perfect solution: all possible options have advantages and drawbacks. Note also that in many cases, the name provided to you for entry into your database may already have been anglicised, especially if the person has been living for some time in an English-speaking country. If you are really confused, the easiest option will probably be to contact the person and ask which part of the name they want in which field.

If you cannot do this, the easiest strategy is to enter the name in the order in which it was given to you, and use the 'preferred name' field to indicate which name is used for informal address. If you encounter a Tamil name with initials in it, enter these initials under 'given name' and 'middle name' as a temporary measure and contact the person to ask what they stand for.

Given name	Middle name	Surname	Preferred name
Devanapathy	Kunanayagam	Manavalan	Manavalan
Shanmugam		Radhika	Radhika

If the names were provided to you using the s/o and d/o format, the simplest option is to omit the s/o or d/o and enter the names as you would an Anglo-Saxon name.

Given name	Middle name	Surname	Preferred name
Manavalan		Devanapathy	Manavalan
Radhika		Shanmugam	Radhika

Christian Tamil names

Christian Tamil names can be entered into databases in the same way as Anglo-Saxon names. Place whichever of the given names the person prefers to use under 'preferred name'.

	Given name	Middle name	Surname	Preferred name
Female	Esther	Manjula	Ratnasingham	Manjula
Male	James	Ariratnam	Premarajah	James

pronunciation

consonants

The letters **q**, **w**, **x** and **z** are not used in romanised Tamil, and **y** is used only as a vowel. The remaining consonants in romanised Tamil are pronounced roughly as they are in English, though note that in Tamil many of these have *retroflex* versions, where the consonants are pronounced with the tongue curled up and back so that the tip of the tongue is touching the palate behind the front teeth.

c	As in 'cat' (rare in romanised Tamil)	r	Rolled, similar to the Spanish 'r'
g	As in 'gun'	th	Aspirated 't', as in 'tin'

vowels

a	Like 'u' in 'bun'	ee	As in 'meet'
aa, ā	Like 'a' in 'father'	i	As in 'tin'
ai	As in 'aisle'	o	Like 'aw' in 'raw'
au	Like 'ow' in 'how'	oo	As in 'pool'
e	As in 'bet'	u	As in 'put'

common Tamil names

Tamil names tend to be very long, and surnames are not always present. Therefore, rather than a list of the most common surnames, a list of components which may be found within those long names is provided on the following page. When saying the component, place the stress on the syllable in **bold type**.

Component	Approximate pronunciation	Component	Approximate pronunciation
deva	**day**-va	pathy	**pah**-tee
jaya	**jay**-ah	priya	**pree**-yah
kumar	koo-**marr** ('oo' as in book)	ragu	**rah**-goo
maniam	**mah**-nyahm	siva	**see**-vah, **shee**-vah
nathan	**nah**-tn	waran	**wah**-rahn

common Tamil given names

Names listed under 'Younger generation' below are seldom seen in Tamils born before the 1970s, although names listed under 'Older generation' may be seen in people of any age.

	Men	Women
Older generation	Balasubramaniam, Janahan, Logeswaran, Rasaratnam, Soruban	Arunthathy, Dushyanthi, Gowri, Manimehalai, Nalini, Shantha
Younger generation	Balakumar, Kumar, Ravishanka, Sanjeev, Sivakumar, Srikumar	Ananthi, Asha, Manjula, Priya, Rohini, Roshini, Shanthi, Sharmilla

chapter 14
Sinhalese
names

background

about the Sinhalese language

Sinhalese, also known as *Sinhala*, is the national language of Sri Lanka, spoken as a first language by about two-thirds of the population. It is derived from Sanskrit, and belongs to the Indo-Aryan family of languages spoken in the north of India, rather than the Dravidian languages spoken in neighbouring southern India.

Sinhalese is written using an abugida (see page 22) called *Sinhala* or *Sinhala akuru*, which consists of 36 basic symbols. These symbols are all curved in shape, which is thought to be because Sinhalese, like Tamil, was originally written on palm leaves, which tended to split when straight lines were written on them using a stylus. As there is no established romanisation system, the spelling of words and names in romanised Sinhalese can vary, and may not be a clear guide to pronunciation.

about Sinhalese names

Sinhalese names traditionally begin with a gē name. Gē, pronounced similar to the word 'gay', is a Sinhalese word that means something like 'from the house of' or 'from the tribe of', and it is placed after the name of the traditional occupation or tribe of the family. For example, if the head of the family was a teacher, or 'guru', the gē name would be 'Guruge' (sometimes written Guru Ge). The ge name was traditionally placed first, before the given names and surname.

The gē name is now becoming obsolete. Centuries of European colonisation, starting with the Portuguese in the 16th century, followed by the Dutch and English, have led to a majority of Sinhalese people adopting the Westernised given name + surname structure. In many cases the family's gē name was converted into a surname by shifting it to the end, leading to the large proportion of Sinhalese surnames which end with -ge or -ke. In other cases, families adopted European surnames, such as de Silva and Gomes from the Portuguese, and Vantwist from the Dutch. It is now becoming popular for families with Portuguese and Dutch surnames to replace them with the gē name, often after removing gē or lage from the end. For example, Widenalage Amali Perera might change her name to 'Amali Widane'.

The minority of families who retain a gē name today typically use it only on very official documents, like birth certificates. People from these families may have five names: the father's gē name, the mother's gē name, two given names and a surname—each more than 10 letters long!

Most Sinhalese people are Buddhists. Children born into a Buddhist family are taken to an astrologer, who uses the time and place of birth to come up with a short list of auspicious initials for the child's given name. Most families will then consult with a scholar or book of names to help them select a meaningful name with good associations starting with one of these letters.

Fashions in Sinhalese names have changed considerably over the last century. Before Sri Lanka gained independence in 1948, many people selected English given names. This fashion gradually gave way to Sanskrit names popular in northern India, such as Rashmi and Suresh, but since about 1990 there has been a swing back to pure Sinhalese names, like Asoke and Ransiri.

structure

examples of Sinhalese names

Most Sinhalese people structure their names like Anglo-Saxon names, with a given name, middle name and surname. The gē name, if present, is placed before the given name, though most Sinhalese omit it in English-speaking contexts.

	Given name	2nd given name	Surname
Female	නිලුකා	මාලා	සෙනෙවිරත්න
	Niluka	Mala	Senawiratne
Male	ළසන්ත	පියුම්	පෙරේරා
	Lasantha	Pium	Perera

addressing Sinhalese people

Sinhalese names are used in the same way as Anglo-Saxon names, with the title + surname used for formal address, and given name used for informal address.

	Formal address	Informal address
Female	Ms Senawiratne	Niluka (or Nilu, etc.)
Male	Mr Perera	Lasantha (or Las, etc.)

Sinhalese titles

Sinhalese titles are placed *after* the family name, hence Senawiratne Menaviya, Perera Mahathya.

Title	English equivalent
Mahattaya	Mr (used in writing)
Mahathya	Mr (used in speech)
Menaviya	Miss (pronounced me-na-*wee*-ya)
Mahathmiya	Mrs

wives and children

Sinhalese women typically replace their surname with their husband's after marriage, though a small number may add their husband's surname onto the end of their name instead. If the woman has a gē name, however, she retains it after marriage.

Children take their father's surname.

anglicising Sinhalese names

Most modern Sinhalese names have the same structure as Anglo-Saxon names, and do not need to be anglicised, apart from omitting the gē name, if present. Due to the great length of Sinhalese names, however, you may see people dropping their middle names or shortening their given names to make them easier to use in English-speaking contexts.

entering Sinhalese names in a database

A typical Sinhalese name can be entered in the same way as an Anglo-Saxon name, with any shortened nicknames placed under 'preferred name'. Note, however, that Sinhalese names can be very long: a database in which Sinhalese names are entered should allow for this and make sure each field can accommodate at least 16 letters.

	Given name	Middle name	Surname	Preferred name
Female	Niluka	Shalini	Senawiratne	Nilu
Male	Lasantha	Pium	Perera	Las

If a gē name is present, the issue becomes more complex. A possible solution that will result in the name being printed out in correct order is: place the gē name under 'given name', the last part of the name under 'surname', any other names under 'middle name', and the given name used for informal address under 'preferred name'. For example, Mudianselage Renuka Lalanthi Fernandes could be entered as shown on the next page.

In this situation, the best thing to do is to contact the person for advice: in many cases, Sinhalese people are happy to use just given name + surname (e.g. Renuka Fernandes) in English-speaking contexts.

Given name	Middle name	Surname	Preferred name
Mudianselage	Renuka Lalanthi	Fernandes	Renuka

pronunciation

consonants

The letters **q**, **x** and **z** are not used in romanised Sinhalese.

c	As in 'cat'	t	Unaspirated 't', as in 'stop'
d	Unaspirated 'd', as in 'study'	th	Aspirated 't', as in 'top'
g	As in 'go'	v	As in 'vat', except when followed by 'i' or 'o', in which case it is pronounced like 'w' in 'wax'
r	Slightly rolled	w	As in 'wax'

vowels

When an **a** or an **e** falls on a stressed syllable, it is pronounced as shown in the example below. When it falls on an unstressed syllable, it is pronounced like the sound **uh**. For example, the common surname Samarawickrama is pronounced '**sah**-muh-ruh-**wick**-ruh-muh'.

a	As in 'father'	i	Like 'ee' in 'bee'
ai	As in 'aisle'	o	As in 'bore'
au	Like the 'ow' in 'cow'	u	As in 'put'
e	As in 'hey'		

common Sinhalese surnames

The following surnames are common among the Sinhalese. Note that surnames of Portuguese origin are often found in Sri Lanka; these were often adopted after conversion to Christianity.

Sinhalese origin	Gunawardena, Jayasuriya, Jayawardena, Ranatunga, Samarawickrama, Weerasooriya, Wickramasinghe, Witarena
Former gē names	Anything ending in -ge or -ke (e.g. Liyanage); 'la' or 'le' often precedes the -ge or -ke, as in Mudianselage, Karunatileke
Portuguese origin	de Silva, de Sousa, de Soysa, Dias, Fernandes, Gomes, Perera

The length of Sinhalese surnames can often be intimidating for English speakers. A good way to make them less daunting is to cut them into shorter components, such as those shown in the examples that follow.

Component	Approximate pronunciation	Component	Approximate pronunciation
abey	ah + bay	singhe	Like the word 'singer'
banda	bun + dah	sooriya	soo + ree + yah
jaya	jay + yah	wardena	'wa' in 'war' + deh + nah
ratna	rut + nah	weera	wee + rah
samara	sah + muh + ruh	wickrama	wick + ruh + ma

common Sinhalese given names

Most Sinhalese given names are gendered. Often there is a male version of a name ending in -a or a consonant (e.g. Lasantha, Vidusha, Upul); and a female version ending in -i (e.g. Lasanthi, Vidushi, Upuli). Names ending in -i tend to be female, but names ending in -a may be male or female.

There are also some unisex names. In some cases, the name will be written the same way for both sexes, but pronounced one way for a man and another for a woman. For example, if the final a in 'Asoka' is pronounced ah, the person is a woman; if it is pronounced uh, the person is a man.

	Men	Women
Older generation	Aravinda, Chandra (unisex), Kamal, Lalith, Nandasiri, Sarat, Sudat, Tissa	Anula, Chitra, Kamala, Setha, Prema, Ranjanie
Younger generation	Chatura, Dimantha, Jayamal, Prabath, Raveen, Thavindu	Amali, Amanthi, Janaki, Lalanthi, Nimali, Sarini,

chapter 15
Pakistani
names

about the Urdu language

The national language of Pakistan is *Urdu*, although it is only the first language of about eight per cent of the population. Although Urdu is used in schools, most people grow up speaking one of the smaller regional languages of Pakistan, notably the four official languages of the provinces of Pakistan: *Punjabi* in the province of Punjab, *Pushto* in the NWFP (North-West Frontier Province), *Sindhi* in Sindh, and *Balochi* in Balochistan. English is also widely used, especially in office correspondence.

There is some debate about the origin and nature of Urdu. Urdu developed in the north-west of the Indian subcontinent around the 17th century, during the rule of the Mughuls, who reigned from 1526 to 1858. It combines vocabulary from Persian (*Farsi*) and Turkish brought in from further west by the Mughuls with the vocabulary and grammar of the local languages of this area, which are referred to collectively by linguists as *Hindustani*. Because Urdu and Hindi share the same grammar and are mutually intelligible at a colloquial level, some scholars argue that they should be considered dialects of the same language. Other scholars, especially those in Pakistan, argue against this on the grounds that the languages have different vocabulary at a formal level and use a different script.

Urdu is written using a 36-symbol abjad (see page 24) called *Nastaliq*, which was developed by Usman, the fourth caliph. Nastaliq is a modified version of the Arabic abjad with extra symbols and alterations added to represent Urdu sounds which are not present in Arabic.

There is no official romanisation system for Urdu, although the widespread use of English has led to established spellings for many words and names.

about Pakistani names

There are notable differences between the four provinces of Pakistan in terms of the names used. In Punjab, the most populous province, most people have one or two given names followed by a subcaste name, which may sometimes be dropped from the name for common use. The names of most people in the NWFP end in Khan, which was originally an old Mongolian title meaning 'leader'. In Sindh and Balochistan, people usually have two given names follwed by the name of their tribe.

Given names are usually chosen by the eldest relatives on the father's side of the family, though other family members may also have input. Pakistanis consider it important to select a name which has a good meaning as well as a good sound. Various methods may be used for selecting an appropriate name. An old tradition is to open the Qur'an at a random page and give the child a name beginning with the first letter on that page, though this practice is dwindling, especially in the cities. Another popular option is to consult with a scholar for advice. Some families may do their own research to find a name which is melodious and meaningful, and some may name their children after movie stars.

Boys are usually given at least one name of religious origin. The most common religious name is Muhammad, the name of the Prophet, but there are many others. God has 99 names in Islam, and these often precede the name Abdul, which means 'servant of'. For example, Musawar means 'painter', and refers to the aspect of God that has brought life and colour to the world; Abdul Musawar could be used in a man's name. Other popular religious names include the names of Muhammad's descendents and companions, the names of other Prophets who preceded Muhammad, such as Musa (Moses), Ibrahim (Abraham) and Isa (Jesus), and the names of caliphs, especially Usman, Umar and Ali.

Girls may not have any names of religious origin, partly because much fewer female religious names exist. Religious female names are mostly taken from the wives and female descendents of Muhammad, notably his wives Khadija and Aisha and his daughters Fatima and Ruqiya. Other girls' names are often references to flowers or 'feminine' virtues such as beauty, grace and gentleness.

structure

examples of Pakistani names

Pakistani men usually have at least one Arabic given name of religious significance. This is usually placed before the given name they use for informal address.

This given name may also be religious, but it could also be a non-religious name derived from Arabic, Farsi or Sanskrit. The male example below illustrates this, with the name of the Prophet, Muhammad, used as a religious name, and the non-religious Arabic name Arif used as the given name. The tribe or subcaste name is similar to the English surname and is usually placed on the end.

Among Pakistani women, religious names are less common. Instead, women often include their father's given name, as shown in the female example below. **Yusuf** is Arabic for 'Joseph'.

		Given name	Father's given name	Tribe or subcaste name
Female	Urdu	فرح	يوسف	خان
	romanised	Farah	Yusuf	Khan
		Religious name	Given name	Tribe or subcaste name
Male	Urdu	محمد	عارف	قریشی
	romanised	Muhammad	Arif	Qureshi

There are also various other name structures among Pakistanis. Some tribe or subcaste names that were originally titles, such as **Mirza** and **Malik**, may be placed at the beginning of the name as well as at the end. You may also encounter Pakistani women whose names begin with her father's given name and contains no tribe or subcaste name. Examples of these types of names are shown below.

	Tribe or subcaste name	Religious name	Given name
Surname first, male	Mirza	Usman	Tahir
	Father's given name	**Religious name**	**Given name**
No surname, female	Nadeem	Sayyeda	Maryam

addressing Pakistani people

As a general rule, Pakistanis prefer to be addressed by title + tribe or subcaste name for formal address and by given name for informal address. However, the range of possible structures used for Pakistani names can make it difficult to establish which part of the name is which. If in doubt, ask the person what they prefer

	Formal address	Informal address
Female	Ms Khan	Farah
Male	Mr Qureshi, Mr Arif*	Arif
Male, surname first	Mr Mirza, Mr Tahir*	Tahir
Female, no surname	Ms Nadeem	Maryam

*Mr Qureshi and Mr Mirza are more likely to be used, but Mr Arif and Mr Tahir are also possible, depending on personal preference.

Urdu titles

In Pakistan, the Anglo-Saxon titles Mr, Mrs and Miss are often used rather than the Urdu titles listed on the opposite page.

174

Urdu title	Comments
Jannab	Equivalent of Mr, used before the given name for adult men, e.g. Jannab Arif; can also be used on its own like 'Sir'
Saheb	Equivalent of Mr, more commonly used than Jannab; placed after the given name, e.g. Arif Saheb
Saheba	Equivalent of Ms, used for adult women regardless of marital status; placed after the given name, e.g. Farah Saheba
Begum	Old term for 'wife of', used with a woman's husband's given name, e.g. Begum Arif; now almost obsolete as a title

wives and children

After marriage, Pakistani women typically replace their own tribe or caste name with their husband's. If the woman's name contains her father's given name, she may also change this to her husband's given name. For example, if Farah Yusuf Khan were to marry Muhammad Arif Qureshi, she might change her name to Farah Arif Khan or Farah Yusuf Qureshi. The latter is more likely.

Children usually inherit their father's tribe or subcaste name, though not always. Sometimes children also have their father's given name in their names: for example, the daughter of Farah and Arif might be called Kiran Arif Qureshi. It is also possible for children not to have any part of their father's name, as might be the case in a Punjabi family where the father's family has dropped the subcaste name from the end.

anglicising Pakistani names

Pakistanis do not generally adapt their names for use in English-speaking contexts. However, you may sometimes see people informally omitting the given name that they do not use for address and using their given name with their tribe or subcaste name (or the father's given name, if there is no tribe or subcaste name) as a surname; that is, Farah Khan, Arif Qureshi, Tahir Mirza and Maryam Nadeem.

entering Pakistani names in databases

The most practical way to enter Pakistani names into a Western database is exactly as you would enter a three-part Anglo-Saxon name, using the 'preferred name' field to indicate the name which the person uses for informal address.

Even if the tribe or subcaste name used as a 'surname' is placed first, it should end up in the right place provided you ensure your forms ask for a 'family name'. Most Pakistanis will understand that this is where they should enter their tribe or subcaste name. However, you may need to be careful when including the person's full name on official documents, as in these situations they will probably want the original order restored. If in doubt, ask the person.

	Given name	Middle name	Surname	Preferred name
Female	Farah	Yusuf	Khan	Farah
Male	Muhammad	Arif	Qureshi	Arif

	Given name	Middle name	Surname	Preferred name
Surname first, male	Usman	Tahir	Mirza	Tahir
No surname, female	Sayyeda	Maryam	Nadeem	Maryam

pronunciation

consonants

Consonants not listed below are pronounced as they are in English.

ch	As in 'chip'	q	Like 'k' in 'kit'
gh	Like 'ch' in 'loch'* (gutteral 'h' sound in the back of the throat)	r	Rolled, similar to the Spanish 'r'
kh	As above		

*If you cannot say this, use 'g' as in 'girl'.

vowels

a	As in 'father' (when stressed; otherwise 'uh')	i	Like 'ee' in 'bee'
ai	As in 'rain' *or* as in 'aisle'	o	Like the word 'awe'
au	Like 'ow' in 'how'	u	As in 'put' *or* as in 'bun'
e	Like 'e' in 'get' but a bit longer		

common Pakistani family names

Different family names are common in the four different provinces of Pakistan.

Province	Common tribe or subcaste names
Punjab	Baigh, Malik, Mirza, Niazi, Pervaiz, Qureshi
NWFP	Khan (shared by almost all people from NWFP)
Sindh	Bhatti, Bhutto, Janjua, Jatoi, Karzai
Balochistan	Baloch, Bugti, Marri, Mengal

common Pakistani given names

In these tables, 'Younger generation' refers to people born in the 1970s or later.

male

Older generation	Abdullah, Alaudin, Charagh Din, Din Muhammad, Ditta, Mustafa, Nadeem, Usman
Younger generation	Ali, Babar, Fawad, Khurram, Mumtaz, Nadeem, Tahir, Yasir

female

Older generation	Fatima, Jannat, Khadeeja, Khudaija, Nasreen, Parveen, Ruksana
Younger generation	Aisha, Farah, Fauziah, Irum, Kiran, Maria, Noreen, Sameena, Sumaira

chapter 16
Bangladeshi names

background

about the Bangla language

Bangladesh was originally part of a larger region called
Bengal, where a language called *Bengali* was spoken. In
1947, the British partitioned the subcontinent into two
separate states, the predominantly Hindu India and the
predominantly Muslim Pakistan. The western part of
Bengal remained part of India, but the eastern part became
the province of East Pakistan.

Although both parts of Pakistan were predominantly
Muslim, as planned by the British, the large geographical
and cultural separation of the western and eastern
parts of Pakistan caused conflict, and the eastern part
ultimately broke away and became the independent state
of Bangladesh in 1971.

The Bengali spoken as a first language by about 90 per
cent of the people in this new country was officially renamed
Bangla, and made the official language of Bangladesh.

There are minor differences between Bengali and Bangla in vocabulary and pronunciation, but essentially they are regional dialects of the same language.

Like Bengali, Bangla is written in the *Bangla Barnamala* script. This is an abugida (see page 22) in which the symbols are arranged in logical order, with the vowels first, followed by the consonants, semivowels and diphthongs. Bangla Barnamala was derived from Sanskrit, but contains some Perso-Arabic influences from Islam and many words borrowed from English.

Bangla contains some sounds and distinctions which are difficult to represent using the Roman alphabet. There is no standard system of romanisation for Bangla, and several spellings of common Bangla names and words exist in many cases, some of which may be poor representations of the actual pronunciation.

about Bangla names

This chapter explains the names of Muslim Bangladeshis, who comprise about 85 per cent of the population. Note that the Hindu minority follow different naming customs, which tend to be more similar in structure to Hindi names.

Bangladeshi Muslims have either two or three names, of which the last is a family name. This family name may be one of the father's names, an old tribal name or an old honorary title, like Kazi, which means 'judge'. Unlike Anglo-Saxon 'surnames', the Bangladeshi 'family name' is not necessarily passed down from father to children in a consistent pattern.

The given name is placed before the family name, and is used for personal address. When choosing a child's given name, Bangladeshis typically invite input from a range of people, notably the grandparents, but also other friends and relatives. Given names may be Bangla or Arabic in origin. Names of Bangla origin may be taken from Bangla literature, selected from a names book or dictionary, or simply chosen after discussion with friends and relatives. Names of Arabic origin are usually religious in meaning and they are commonly chosen in consultation with an Islamic scholar. Another custom which may be used is opening the Qur'an to a random page and choosing a name which begins with the first letter on that page.

Many Bangladeshis also have a 'name prefix' before their given name, which is not used for address. The name prefix is often either an old honorary title, such as **Khan**, which means 'leader', or a name with religious meaning. Among men, the name of the Prophet (spelt 'Mohammad' in Bangladesh) is a common name prefix; there is also a version of Mohammad given as a name prefix to women, 'Mosammat'. Male names almost always contain a name prefix; most female names do not. The name prefix may be shared by other family members, especially siblings of the same sex.

structure

examples of Bangla names

The standard Bangladeshi name contains three parts: a name prefix, a personal name and a family name. The name prefix is usually either a religious name, like 'Mohammad', or an old title, such as **Kazi**, meaning 'judge', or as above, **Khan**, meaning 'leader'. Male names almost always contain a name prefix; a strong minority of female names do not. The name prefix may be shared by other family members, especially siblings of the same sex.

The personal name is the name by which people are addressed. This name is often shortened to form an informal nickname. The family name is shared by other family members, although it is not always passed down from the father to the children in the manner of Anglo-Saxon names. Sometimes children may use their father's given name as a family name. It is also common for female family members to have a different family name from male family members. For example, one Bangladeshi man I interviewed told me that he and his brothers shared the family name Zaman, but his sisters all shared the family name Akhter instead.

		Name prefix	Personal name	Family name
Male	Bangla	কাজি	আজিজুর	রহমান
	romanised	Kazi	Azizur	Rahman
Female	Bangla	মোছাম্মাৎ	ফিরোজা	খানম
	romanised	Mosammat	Firoza	Khanam

addressing Bangladeshi people

English speakers typically use title + family name when addressing Bangladeshis formally. This is because the family name is last and therefore resembles the Anglo-Saxon surname. Bangladeshis themselves use title + personal name rather than title + family name, but in English-speaking contexts they usually follow local customs.

When addressing a Bangladeshi informally, the personal name is used. Note that men's personal names which end in **-ur** drop the **-ur** in spoken form. For example, Azizur would be shortened to Aziz, as shown in the diagram below.

	Formal address	Informal address
Male	Mr Rahman	Aziz
Female	Ms Khanam	Firoza

Bangla titles

The titles Jannab and Jannaba may sometimes be spelt 'Jannaab' and 'Janaaba'. Note that Hindu Bangladeshis use different titles: Sri for Mr, Srimati for Mrs and Kumari for Miss, placed before the surname.

Muslim titles	Comments
Jannab	Mr; precedes given name (Jannab Aziz)
Jannaba	Mrs; precedes given name (Jannaba Firoza)
Shaheb	Mr; follows given name (Aziz Shaheb). Seldom used as a title, but often used by itself to mean 'sir'
Saheba	Miss; follows given name (Firoza Saheba), but almost never used
Apa	Big sister; Used by itself to address a young woman older than the speaker, meaning 'madam' or 'miss'

Muslim titles	Comments
Apu	Little sister. Used by itself to address a girl or young woman younger than the speaker, meaning 'madam' or 'miss'
Madam	The English word 'madam' is generally used for older women

wives and children

There are few definite rules about the names of wives and children in Bangladesh: many different possibilities are seen.

Some Bangladeshi women do not change their names after marriage; others replace their family name with their husband's family name. For example, if the two people given as examples in this chapter were to marry, Firoza might change her name to Mosammat Firoza Rahman. Other less likely options include replacing her name prefix with her husband's (Kazi Firoza Khanam), or replacing her family name with her husband's name prefix (Mosammat Firoza Kazi).

Children's names often incorporate either their father's family name or his name prefix or both. For example, the son of Aziz and Firoza might be called Kazi Atikur Rahman, inheriting both his father's family name and name prefix. Daughters sometimes inherit part of their mother's name instead. In the last decade or so, it has also become common to find children's names that have not inherited any part of their parents' names.

anglicising Bangla names

In English-speaking contexts, Bangladeshis may informally drop their name prefix, producing a name that can be used in the same way as a standard Anglo-Saxon given name + surname structure. Bangladeshis also commonly use nicknames and short versions of their personal name among themselves, which fortuitously makes them easier for English speakers to use as well.

entering Bangla names in a database

Bangladeshi names can be entered into a Western database in the same way as an Anglo-Saxon name. As this will place the personal name used for informal address under 'middle name', it is important to enter it under 'preferred name' to make the correct use of the name clear. If the name used for informal address is a nickname or shortened name, like 'Aziz', this should be entered under 'preferred name' instead.

	Given name	Middle name	Surname	Preferred name
Male	Azizur	Rahman	Kazi	Aziz
Female	Mosammat	Firoza	Khanam	Firoza

pronunciation

Although there is no consistent romanisation system for Bangla, the established spellings were designed by the

British, and letters are therefore generally pronounced in the same way as they are in English.

vowels

a	As in 'father'	i	Like 'ee' in 'bee'
ai	As in 'aisle' or as in 'rain'	o	Like 'aw' in 'raw'
e	As in 'jet'	u	As in 'put'
ee	Like 'ay' in 'day'		

consonants

ch	As in 'chip'	s	Like 's' in 'sand' or 'sh' in 'shell'
j	As in 'jam', but softer	th	Like the aspirated 't' in 'top'
kh	Similar to 'k' in 'kit'	z	Between a 'j' and a 'z'
q	Like 'k' but more gutteral		

common name prefixes

Most common name prefixes are either religious, like 'Mohammad', or were originally titles—for example, **Kazi**, which is an old word for 'judge', **Khan**, which originally meant 'leader' and **Sheikh**, which refers to a 'merchant lord'.

Unisex name prefixes	Male name prefixes	Female name prefixes
Khan, Sheikh	Kazi, Miah, Mohammad, Shah, Syed	Mosammat, Sayeeda

common personal names

The following personal names are common in Bangladesh.

Male personal names	Female personal names
Abidur, Anisur, Atikur, Azizur, Bashar, Habib, Harun, Khaled, Mashud, Nazmul, Omar, Rahim, Rashid, Sagar	Fatima, Firoza, Gulshan, Habiba, Humaira, Jannat, Khadeza, Mamtaz, Mariam, Nargis, Rabia, Shahina, Shirin

common family names

Some of the male personal names listed in the above table may also be used as family names.

Unisex family names	Female-only family names
Chaklader, Chowdhury, Ferdeoz, Haque, Hossain, Hussan, Islam, Khan, Malik, Miah, Mollah, Rahman	Akhter, Ara, Begum, Khanam, Parvin, Sultana

chapter 17
Malay
names

background

about the Malay language

Malay was originally a spoken language used for trade in
Peninsular Malaysia, Borneo and much of the Indonesian
archipelago. When Indonesia was federated in 1949, the
language spoken across the islands it encompassed was
renamed *Bahasa Indonesia* (Indonesian) and the language
spoken in Malaysia continued to be called Malay.
Indonesian and Malay are effectively the same language,
though there are regional variations in language, accent
and vocabulary.

The Arabs who came to Malaysia for the spice trade
in the 15th and 16th centuries used Arabic script to write
Malay, and there are a few publications in Malaysia which
still do so. However, the romanised script established by
the British colonists in the 19th and 20th centuries is now
the official system used to write Malay.

There are three major ethnic groups in Malaysia and

Singapore. The Malays, comprising about 55 per cent of the population in Malaysia and 15 per cent in Singapore, are Muslims, a growing number of whom study Arabic so that they can read the Qur'an in its original language. The Chinese, comprising about 30 per cent of the population in Malaysia and 77 per cent in Singapore, originate primarily from south-eastern China and speak languages from this region, notably *Hokkien*, *Cantonese*, *Hakka* and *Teo Chew*. The Indians, comprising about ten per cent of the population in Malaysia and six per cent in Singapore, are mostly *Tamil* speakers from the Indian state of Tamil Nadu.

about Malay names

Arab traders brought Islam to the Malay people in the 9th century, and with the religion came Islamic names. Although few Malays use the complex five-part names seen in parts of the Middle East, they do select names from the Qur'an (usually spelt 'Koran' by Malays) and follow the Arabic custom of using the father's name to indicate family relationships rather than having some form of family name.

In Malaysia, the father's name is preceded by **bin**, which means 'son of', or **binti**, which means 'daughter of' (sometimes this is spelt binte). Note that bin and binti are often abbreviated to b. and bt. respectively. Malays also commonly use 'name prefixes', which are names placed before the given name and have religious significance. These may sometimes be abbreviated: for example, 'Mohamad' is often used as a name prefix, and it is usually abbreviated to 'Mohd.', 'Md.' or 'Mhd'. Other name prefixes are listed in this chapter under 'Common names'.

As with all Muslims, people who have made a pilgrimage to Mecca are honoured by adding the title **Haji** for men or **Hajjah** for women (sometimes shortened to **Hj.**) to the front of their names. People who convert to Islam often adopt an Arabic name which sounds similar to their own. For example, Hans might adopt the new name Mohamad Hanif.

structure

examples of Malay names

As shown in these examples, the father's full name, including name prefix, is usually included in a Malay name.

	Name prefix	Given name	Patronymic	Father's name prefix	Father's given name
Male	Syed	Rizwan	bin		Faisal
Female	Siti	Aminah	binti	Mohd.	Razeleigh

addressing Malay people

In Malaysia, the correct way to address people is title + given name (e.g. Mr Rizwan and Ms Aminah). However, English-speaking people almost always assume that the last part of a Malay name is the 'surname' and use it with the title, as they would in English; this is still an acceptable form of address in English-speaking contexts.

	Formal address	Informal address
Male	Mr Faisal/Mr Rizwan	Rizwan
Female	Ms Razeleigh/Miss Aminah	Aminah

If the person has a more specialised title, such as **Haji**, **Tengku** or any of the others listed under 'Honorary titles' and 'Hereditary titles' on the next page, this should be used with the given name instead.

Malay titles

Malay titles are placed before the given name (e.g. Encik Rizwan, Hajjah Aminah). Remember that people raised in Asia tend to be a lot more status-oriented than people raised in English-speaking countries, and it is very important to show appropriate respect to people of high status. People with one of the honorary or hereditary titles listed below should be addressed by these titles. Usually such people will have an entourage with them, and it is best to ask someone in that entourage about the correct form of address. Otherwise, address the person as 'Sir' or 'Madam' and politely ask what they would prefer.

general titles

The following general titles are used in Malaysia. Where there is a standard abbreviation for a title, this is shown beneath the full title in parentheses. If a person's father has visited Mecca, Haji or Hj. would be included in their name after bin or binti, e.g. Noraini bt. Haji Sulaiman.

Title	English equivalent	Title	English equivalent
Encik	Mr	Doktor (Dr)	Dr
Cik	Ms (younger women)	Haji (Hj.)	Honorary title for men who have made the pilgrimage to Mecca
Puan	Mrs	Hajjah (Hjh.)	Honorary title for women who have made the pilgrimage to Mecca

honorary titles

There are a number of titles that may be awarded to Malaysian citizens for services to their country or state. Tun, Tan Sri and Datuk, in descending order of prestige, are Federal titles awarded by the ruler of Malaysia. Dato Sri Utama, Dato Sri and Dato', in descending order of prestige, are state titles awarded by the sultan or hereditary ruler of a Malaysian state. An alternative spelling of Sri you may see is 'Seri'.

Note that when a man receives one of these titles, his wife automatically receives the corresponding wife's title in the right-hand column. If a woman is awarded one of these titles, her husband does not receive a title.

Title	Wife's title
Tun	Toh Puan
Tan Sri	Puan Sri
Datuk	Datin
Dato Sri Utama	Datin Sri Utama

Title	Wife's title
Dato Sri/Datuk Paduka	Datin Sri
Dato'/Datuk	Datin/Toh Puan

hereditary titles

These titles are passed down through families. Note that people with these titles should be addressed either by title alone (**Tengku**), or by title + personal name (Tengku **Nina**). Note that **Said/Syed** and **Sharifah** may not always be hereditary titles as was the case traditionally: it is becoming common to choose these as given names.

Title	Meaning
Tunku/Tengku	Prince/Princess: child of a sultan
Said/Syed (m), Sharifah (f)	Descendant of the Prophet
Sheikh	Descendant of a merchant lord

wives and children

Malay women do not change their names after marriage. However, if their husband has an honorary title, they will assume the corresponding wife's honorary title when they marry, as shown above. For example, if a Malay woman married a **Tan Sri**, she would automatically be granted the title **Puan Sri**.

Children take **bin** (for boys) or **binti** (for girls) + their father's given name. For example, Nurul-Huda, the daughter of Abdullah bin Mohamad, would be Nurul-Huda binti Abdullah. Note that if the child's father has an honorary title, they may include this (e.g. Ali bin Dato Abdullah). If the child's father has a hereditary title, this will be placed in front of the given names of both child and father (e.g. Tengku Ali bin Tengku Abdullah).

Note as previously mentioned that **bin** may be shortened to **b.**, and **binti** (old spelling **binte**) may be shortened to **bt.** You may occasionally see Malay equivalents of these terms, which are **a/l**, short for **anak lelaki** (son of), and **a/p**, short for **anak perempuan** (daughter of).

anglicising Malay names

In English-speaking contexts, Malay people usually nominate a 'surname' for administrative purposes. Almost all of them use their father's given name, as this is what most English speakers will assume is their surname anyway. Many Malays also drop the **bin** or **binti** from their names (e.g. Syed Rizwan Faisal and Siti Aminah Mohd. Razeleigh).

Although the use of name prefixes can be confusing for English speakers, Malays usually retain these as they have religious significance. Name prefixes may be either written in full (e.g. Mohamad) or abbreviated (e.g. Mohd.).

entering Malay names in a database

The use of name prefixes and *patronymics* makes it difficult to enter Malay names into a Western database. If **bin/binti** is present (and remember many Malays drop this overseas), I would recommend entering it as a 'middle name', with all names before it placed in the 'given name' field and all names after it (the father's name) placed in the 'surname' field, as shown in the first two examples below. Note that this means most mail-merge programs will print labels addressed to 'Ms Mohamad Razeleigh': if you wish to have them addressed to 'Ms Razeleigh', you can place only 'Razeleigh' under 'surname' and put either 'binti Mohamad' or just 'Mohamad' (dropping binti) under 'middle name' as shown in the third example.

The name used for informal address should be placed under 'preferred name' to ensure that the person does not get addressed by the name prefix.

Title	Given name	Middle name	Surname	Preferred name
Mr	Syed Rizwan	(bin)	Faisal	Rizwan
Ms	Siti Aminah	(binti)	Mohamad Razeleigh	Aminah
Ms	Siti Aminah	(binti) Mohamad	Razeleigh	Aminah

If **bin/binti** is not present, use the list of 'Name prefixes' on the next page to determine which part of the name is the person's given name and which part is their father's name.

pronunciation

Malay names are comparatively easy for English speakers to pronounce. These tables provide a guide to pronouncing the letters where the pronunciation is unexpected or ambiguous.

consonants

c	Like the 'ch' in 'chair'	ng	As in 'singer'
g	As in 'garden'	ngg	As in 'anger'
h	Like an English 'h' but heavier; almost silent at the end of a word	ny	As in 'canyon'
j	As in 'join'	sy	Similar to 'sh' in 'sheep' (except in Syed, which is 'Sye-eed')
k	Like an English 'k', when found at the end of a word as a glottal stop (i.e. stop sharply after saying the vowel, as in the Cockney pronunciation of the word 'pot'.	r	Rolled, like a Spanish 'r'

vowels

a	As in 'father'	i	Like the 'ee' in 'meet'
ai	Like the 'i' in 'line'	o	Like the 'o' in 'rote'
au	Like the 'ow' in 'cow'	u	Like the 'u' in 'flute'
e	Stressed, like 'a' in 'may'; unstressed, like 'e' in 'bet'	ua	Like 'ua' in 'guava'

common Malay names

Most Malay names are of Arabic origin, although adapted English names have also been popular since the 1980s, especially for girls.

name prefixes

These are placed before the given name, and have a religious meaning.

Male	Mohamad (Mohd.), Syed/Said (Sy.), Abdul* (Abd.)
Female	Siti, Nur/Noor/Nor**

*Note that 'Abdul' means 'servant of', and must be followed by one of the 99 names of God, such as Rahman, Rahim or Aziz.
**Nur, which means 'light', is often incorporated into the given name (e.g. Noraini, Nurul-Huda).

given names

Many traditional Malay female names end in **-ah** or **-a**. Some may also end in i, like Noraini. More recently, middle-class urban people have begun giving their daughters Malaysianised versions of English names, such as Ellisha, Malena, Nadia and Natasha.

Male	Ali, Amin, Azman, Faisal, Hafifi, Ibrahim, Ismail, Jamil, Razak, Rizwan
Female	Aishah, Aminah, Ellisha, Halizah, Lina, Malena, Nadia, Natasha, Noraisha, Nurul-Huda, Sharifah, Zahlera (older generation)

chapter 18
Indonesian
names

background

about the Indonesian language

During the 19th and early 20th centuries, a language called Malay was used for trade in South-East Asia. After World War II, the islands formerly governed by the Dutch were formally declared to be the Republic of Indonesia. Although a range of languages were spoken on the different islands of this new country, the local form of Malay was chosen as the national language, as it was spoken right across the archipelago. This language was renamed *Bahasa Indonesia*, or *Indonesian*, and was registered as the official national language in 1945.

Indonesian is written using the Roman alphabet. The first people to romanise Indonesian were the Dutch, whose system was used for several decades. In the 1970s, however, the government decided that Indonesia should change over to the British system used for romanising

Malay in Malaysia, and the Dutch-influenced spelling of words like Soeharto and Djakarta were changed to Suharto and Jakarta.

The influence of Islam is also evident in the Indonesian language. The vocabulary of Indonesian includes many borrowings from Arabic, and the Arabic abjad (see page 24) is sometimes used to transcribe Indonesian instead of the Roman alphabet, particularly in devout Islamic regions such as Aceh.

about Indonesian names

When discussing Indonesian names, it is important to remember that Indonesia consists of more than 60 islands, many of which have their own language, culture and naming system. As covering all of these is beyond the scope of this book, this chapter focuses on Javanese Indonesian names, as Java is where the capital of Indonesia, Jakarta, is located, and the Javanese are the most numerous and dominant of the ethnic groups in the archipelago. Note, however, that there is also a local Javanese language, spoken by about 80 per cent of people of Javanese origin, and many names used in Indonesia have their origins in this language.

When a child is born, the parents select a childhood name, which they register with the civil authorities. If misfortune or illness befalls the child before they reach the age of five, the name may be changed and re-registered. Up until the 1960s, when the child attained adulthood by marrying or establishing a career, it was common practice to replace the childhood name with a new name called the nama tua, which was carefully chosen for its meaning and sound.

Before 1970 or so, most people were given names of Sanskrit or ancient Javanese origin. Men were usually given just one name, and women were usually given two. Since then, it has become more usual to give people two or three names, with as many as four occasionally seen. In the 1970s and 1980s it became fashionable to include one or more names of European origin, such as Karina or Eddy. In the 1990s, however, parents began to return to their roots, with Javanese and Sanskrit names regaining popularity, and Arabic names such as Mohamad (the preferred Indonesian spelling of the Prophet's name) becoming more common.

structure

examples of Indonesian names

Indonesians do not usually divide their names into labelled components like 'given name' and 'surname'. They may be confused when they are first asked for these in English-speaking contexts. Although most Indonesians now have two names, you may still encounter Indonesians with only one name (usually men), which can lead to difficulties in English-speaking contexts. (See also the section later in this chapter on databases for further discussion of this issue.)

Unlike the Malays and the Muslims of the Middle East, most Indonesians only include bin (son of) and binti (daughter of) in their names on official civil registration documents for births, deaths and marriages. The Indonesian words putra and putri placed on the end of the father's name, e.g. Bambang Prasetyo Hartonoputra, are now starting to replace the Arabic words bin and binti.

	Name	Name	(indication of father's name)
Male	Bambang	Prasetyo	(bin Hartono *or* Hartonoputra)
Female	Marisa	Sulami	(binti Hadiman *or* Hadimanputri)

addressing Indonesian people

The fluid nature of Indonesian names means that there are no definite rules of address. There is no surname to use with the title, and no given name to use informally. In Indonesia it is most usual to use title + the name that comes first for formal address, and just the first name for informal address, but other variants may be seen. In English-speaking contexts, however, Indonesian people tend to follow Anglo-Saxon custom and use the first name for informal address, and title + the last name for formal address. The best way to manage this ambiguity is to ask the person what they would prefer to be called.

	Formal address possibilities	Informal address possibilities
Male	Mr Bambang, Mr Prasetyo	Bambang, Prasetyo, Pras
Female	Miss Marisa, Ms Sulami	Marisa, Sulami

Indonesian titles

Titles in Indonesian are placed before the preferred name, for example Saudara Bambang, Nona Marisa.

Title	Comments
Saudara	Used to show respect for men of similar age and status or younger; roughly comparable to 'Mr'
Saudari	Used to show respect for women of similar age and status or younger; roughly comparable to 'Ms'
Ibu	Respectful title used for women independent of marital status, usually one older or higher status than the speaker. Literally means 'mother'. Often used by itself to mean 'madam'
Bu	Less formal form of 'ibu'
Bapak	Respectful title used for men independent of marital status, usually one older or higher status than the speaker; often used by itself to mean 'sir'
Pak	Less formal form of 'bapak'
Nyonya	Similar to Mrs: for adult married women
Nona	Similar to Miss: for young unmarried women
Bapak	A respectful form of Mr used when the person being addressed is of higher status than the speaker
Dokter	Doctor, used for medical doctors only; sometimes Pak Dokter is used for male doctors and Bu Dokter for female doctors
Insinyur	A very formal title used for a senior engineer, popular in the 1980s but now becoming less common

wives and children

Indonesian women do not officially change their names after marriage. However, informally they may be known as **Bu** or **Nyonya** followed by their husband's name. For example, if the two Indonesian people in the examples in this chapter were to marry, Marisa might sometimes be known as 'Bu Bambang' or 'Nyonya Bambang', meaning Bambang's wife.

Among the Javanese Indonesians, there is no family name shared by parents and children: children's names usually have no relation to their parents' names at all. Occasionally, 'composite' names may be seen, where the child's name combines elements of both parents' names. For example, Bambang Prasetyo and Marisa Sulami might call their daughter 'Prasmi'.

anglicising Indonesian names

Most Indonesians are relaxed about their names, and are happy to adapt them to make them easier to use. When they come to an English-speaking country, the last part of their name is usually assigned as a 'surname' and the remaining parts as 'given names'. They may also shorten their names to make them easier to pronounce, for example, shortening Susilowati to Susi. Younger Indonesians often have Western names anyway, but those who don't may adopt one for convenience.

Indonesians with only one name will find that they need to use something as a 'surname' in order to function in an English-speaking context.

Many adopt their father's given name as a surname.

Another common option is to enter the same single name under both 'given name' and 'surname', resulting in a double name (e.g. Budiman Budiman).

entering Indonesian names in a database

With databases, the simplest option is to enter the names as if they were Anglo-Saxon names, with the first name under 'given name', the last name under 'surname', and any other names under 'middle name'. The name used for informal address should be entered under 'preferred name'.

	Given name	Middle name	Surname	Preferred name
Male	Bambang		Prasetyo	Bambang, Pras, etc
Female	Marisa		Sulami	Marisa, etc

When entering a name with a single component, one of three options can be used.

If your database allows it, the 'given name' field can be left blank. This is the most correct option, although if you use it, be careful about automatically addressing informal correspondence to 'Dear _____'!

Another possibility for databases that will accept it is to place a punctuation mark, such as a hyphen in the 'given name' field. The advantage of this is that the punctuation mark forms an easily removed placeholder under 'given name' where it is obvious what needs to be removed when printing the name on official documents.

Otherwise, an option accepted by almost all Western databases is putting the name in twice. However, bear in mind that this double name is not the person's official name, and that they may wish to remove the duplicated name if it is to appear on an official document, such as a certificate or reference.

All of these options have advantages and disadvantages: the most important consideration is to find one that your database will accept and *keep it consistent*, with everyone entering data using the same system for managing single names.

Given name	Surname
	Budiman
–	Budiman
Budiman	Budiman

pronunciation

Letters which are not included below are pronounced in the same way as in English.

consonants

c	Like the 'ch' in 'chip'	th	Aspirated 't', as in 'top'
g	As in 'girl'	tj	Like 'ch' in 'chip'
q	Like 'k' in 'kit' (rarely used)	v	Like 'f' in 'fan'
r	Rolled, like the 'r' in Spanish	w	As in 'wax'

vowels

a	As in 'father'	o	Like the word 'awe'
e	As in 'hey'	u	As in 'put'
i	Like 'ee' in 'bee'		

common Indonesian names

Traditionally, Javanese male names often end in -anto, -wan, -man and -di; Javanese female names often end in -anti, -wati, -wo, -ro and -ti. The eras shown below are not absolute. It is possible, for example, that a man called Budiharto may have been born after 1980, but more likely that he was born before 1970.

Era	Men	Women
pre-1970	Bambang, Budiharto, Budiyanto, Gunawan, Hartono, Nanang, Prasang, Setiawan	Hartawati, Herawati, Lasmi, Ratnawati, Sulami, Sulastri, Susilowati
1970–90	Adi, Deddy, Didik, Eddy, Joni, Robert, Simon, Sonny, Tedy	Ami, Cynthia, Erni, Indah, Karina, Luci, Maria, Marisa, Natasha, Yolanda
1990s onwards	Chandra (unisex), Jaya, Krisna, Mohamad, Rama (unisex), Surya	Anisa, Fatima, Kartika, Pramudita, Pritika, Sinta

part three

introduction to part three

Part two of this book is organised by language. This means that in order to know which chapter to consult for a particular name, English speakers first need to know the name's language of origin. Part three, therefore, lists which languages are spoken in Asian countries and provides guidelines on how to identify which language a particular name is likely to be from.

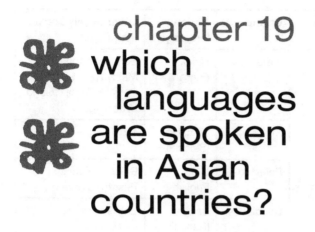

chapter 19
which languages are spoken in Asian countries?

This chapter provides a list of Asian countries, showing the national language in that country, and other languages that are spoken there.

Table 1: Languages spoken in Asian countries

Region	Country	National language/s	Other widely spoken languages
Eastern Asia	China	Mandarin	Cantonese, Shanghainese, others
	Taiwan	Mandarin	Hakka, Taiwanese (also called Hokkien)
	Korea	Korea	–
	Japan	Japanese	–

success with Asian names

Region	Country	National language/s	Other widely spoken languages
South Asia	India	Hindi, English	Bengali, Kannada, Malayalam, Marathi, Punjabi, Tamil, Telugu, Urdu, others
	Sri Lanka	Sinhalese (Sinhala)	Tamil
	Pakistan	Urdu, English	Balochi, Punjabi, Pushto, Sindhi
	Bangladesh	Bangla (Bengali)	English, others
	Myanmar (Burma)	Burmese	English, others
Indo-China	Vietnam	Vietnamese	Hmong, Khmer
	Cambodia	Khmer	Hmong
	Thailand	Thai	Hmong, Khmer, Lao, Malay
	Laos	Lao (Laotian)	Hmong, Thai
South-East Asia	Malaysia	Malay	Cantonese, Hakka, Hokkien, Tamil, Teochew
	Singapore	English, Mandarin, Malay, Tamil	Cantonese, Hakka, Hokkien, Teochew
	Indonesia	Indonesian (Bahasa Indonesia)	Acehnese, Balinese, others

chapter 20
which
language is
this name
from?

It is not possible to develop a foolproof system for identifying the language from which a particular Asian name derives. This is because:

1. some names can belong to more than one cultural group (e.g. the family name 'Lee' can be Korean or Chinese)
2. there will always be a few people whose names are not typical of their cultural group (immigrants, people of mixed origin, people from minority ethnic groups, etc.)
3. many Asians living in a Western country alter the spelling, arrangement and/or use of their name in a way which disguises its origins
4. you may encounter names from cultures which are not covered in this book.

Nonetheless, this chapter will help you start to recognise the characteristics of names from various Asian countries and enable you to narrow down the origins of names at least to two or three possible countries.

Before looking at the tables in this chapter, it is important to note that due to the different romanisation systems used in the countries where Mandarin is spoken, 'Mandarin' is sometimes followed by the country in which the guideline applies. Similarly, where Urdu is listed in these tables, it means the Urdu used in Pakistan, so this is indicated by adding 'Pakistan' in brackets after 'Urdu'. 'Chinese dialects' refers to dialects *other than Mandarin*. Where Hindi is indicated, the same is also likely to be true of the names of Hindus who speak other northern Indian languages such as Gujarati and Marathi.

components

Components are the 'parts' that make up the name, and studying these carefully provides many clues as to the origins of a name.

how many components are there?

The number of components in a name can help determine which language it comes from. For example, names from Japan contain two components (e.g. Shinzata Satoko), whereas Pakistani names contain three components (e.g. Fawad Nadeem Mirza).

Table 2: How many components are there in the name?

Number of components in name	Asian languages where names almost always have this number of components	Asian languages where names sometimes have this number of components
1	–	Indonesian
2	Hindi and other north Indian languages, Japanese, Mandarin (China), Tamil, Thai	Bangla, Punjabi (Sikh), Indonesian, Khmer (Cambodia), Korean, Malay, Sinhalese, Vietnamese
3	Chinese dialects (Cantonese, Hokkien, others), Korean, Mandarin (Singapore, Taiwan), Sinhalese, Urdu (Pakistan)	Indonesian, Malay, Tamil, Vietnamese
4+	–	Malay, Tamil, Vietnamese

how long are the components?

The length of the components in a name can also help the reader determine its country of origin. For example, the components in Tamil names tend to be very long, like 'Thiagurajah', whereas names from Korea tend to be very short with only one syllable, like 'Park'.

Table 3: How long are the components?

	Asian languages where names commonly follow this pattern	Asian languages where names sometimes follow this pattern
All components one syllable long	Chinese dialects, Korean, Mandarin (Taiwan, Singapore), Vietnamese	Khmer
One 1–syllable component; one 2–3 syllable component	Mandarin (China), Sikh	Hindi and other north Indian languages, Indonesian, Japanese, Khmer, Korean, Thai
One or more very long component (more than 8 letters or more than 3 syllables)	Sinhalese, Tamil, Thai	Japanese
Two to three components, all 1–4 syllables in length	Bangla, Hindi, Indonesian, Japanese, Punjabi (Sikh), Sinhalese, Urdu (Pakistan)	Khmer, Tamil

what letters does the name contain?

Another clue to the origins of a name is the letters it contains. For example, the letter **q** is very common in names from Mainland China but is not used at all in Sinhalese names.

Table 4: What letters does the name contain?

	Likely	Possible	Very unlikely to never
q	Bangla, Mandarin, Urdu, Vietnamese	Chinese dialects, Thai	Hindi, Indonesian, Japanese, Korean, Malay, Sikh, Sinhalese, Tamil
th	Hindi, Khmer, Sinhalese, Tamil, Thai, Vietnamese	Bangla, Chinese dialects, Mandarin (Singapore), Sikh, Urdu	Indonesian, Japanese, Korean, Malay, Mandarin (China, Taiwan)
v	Hindi, Khmer, Sikh, Sinhalese, Tamil, Thai, Vietnamese	Indonesian	Chinese dialects, Japanese, Korean, Malay, Mandarin
x	Khmer, Mandarin, Vietnamese	Chinese dialects	Bangla, Hindi, Indonesian, Japanese, Korean, Malay, Sikh, Sinhalese, Tamil, Thai, Urdu

characteristics associated with particular regions or groups

The names covered in this book can be roughly divided into four groups, which share certain features in common. These groups are Confucian names, Indo-Chinese names, Islamic Asian names, and names from the Indian subcontinent.

Confucian names

Names which originate from Chinese languages, Korean and Vietnamese are Confucian names. Most Confucian names contain three one-syllable components, as in names such as Lee Kuan Yew, Kim Jong-Il and Ho Chi Minh, although Mandarin names from Mainland China may contain only two one-syllable components, and Vietnamese names may contain four one-syllable components.

Names from Mainland China usually combine the generation and personal names together to form a two-syllable component, as in the name Deng Xiaoping. This is also occasionally seen among Koreans. Outside China, the generation name and personal name may be either hyphenated (as typically done in Taiwan) or written as separate words.

Table 5: Identifying Confucian names

Language	Components	Syllables	Common components
Mandarin (as used in China)	2	1–2 syllables per component	**Family names:** Huang, Li, Wang, Wu, Zhang, Zhou **Generation/Personal:** Jia, Jun, Lan, Liang, Long, Mei, Ming, Qi, Qiang, Wei, Xiao, Ying, Zi **Names containing:** ei, ian, iao, j, q, x and z
Other Chinese languages	3	1 syllable per component	**Family names:** Cheung, Lau, Lee, Lim, Neoh, Ng, Ong, Tan, Wong **Generation/Personal:** Chin, Chun, Keat, Keng, Mei, Siew/Hsiu, Soo/Su, Swee, Wai **Names containing:** au, hs, iew, ik, ip, ng-, oo

success with Asian names

Language	Components	Syllables	Common components
Korean	2–3, most often 3	1 syllable per component	**Family names:** Cho, Choi, Kim, Lee, Park **Generation/ Personal:** Eun, Hyoung, Hyun, Jae/Chae, Jyun, Mee/Mi, Myoung, Myun, Sook, Sun **Names containing:** ae, eun, hy, jy, my, oung
Vietnamese	2–4, most often 3	1 syllable per component	**Family names:** Dinh, Duong, Le, Nguyen, Pham, Tran, Trinh, Vu **Generation/ Personal:** Bich, Duc, Hong, Hue, Linh, Ly, Mien, Nam, Ngoc, Phuc, Quynh, Thi, Thuy, Van, Xuan **Names containing:** -nh, oa, tr, uong, uy, v

examples of Confucian names

Table 6: Examples of Confucian names

Language	Examples in traditional format	Westernised examples
Mandarin (China)	Li Xiaohua Xu Qingwei Zhou Ming	William Wang Sally Wu Lanping Zhang
Other Chinese languages	Cheung Wing Kit Lim Mei-Ling Neoh Kar Keat	Kitty Cheng Jason Tse Ho Kwan Angelina Ng Sim Lee
Korean	Choi Hyun Ho Kim Sook Mee Lee Pyong Cheol	Chaehyun Cho Su Bin Chung Hee-Sook Park
Vietnamese	Duong Van Trinh Le Thi Ngoc Hoa Tran Dinh Duc	Thuy Le Johnny Nguyen Linh Pham

northern Indian and Indo-Chinese names

Names from northern India and Indo-China both have their origins in Sanskrit, although Chinese has also had a strong influence on names from Indo-China. Names from northern India and Indo-China consist of two or three components. Thai surnames are often very long, containing as many as 18 letters and five syllables or even more; names from the other languages listed in the table below typically contain components which are two or three syllables long.

Table 7: Identifying northern Indian and Indo-Chinese names

Language	Components	Syllables	Common components
Hindi (and other languages spoken by north Indian Hindus)	Usually 2	1–4 per component (usually 2–3)	**Surnames**: Arora, Chandra, Kumar, Lal, Patel/il, Raman, Sharma **Given names containing:** ani, -ash, -esh, -indra, -ini, -man, -mitra, nee, -vati
Punjabi (of Sikh religion)	2 or 3	1–4	**All contain:** Kaur (female) or Singh (male) **Surnames:** Gill, Mann, Sandhu, Grewal, Juneja **Given names containing:** -deep, -inder, -jeet/-jit, -preet, -meet, -veer/vir, gur, prem
Khmer	2 or 3	1–4 (most often 1–2, but 3–4 not uncommon)	**Family names:** Chea, Kong, Noun, Prak, Say, Ung **Names containing:** ath, hh, oeun, pha, sok, soph, tha, thy

Language	Compo-nents	Syllables	Common components
Thai	2	1–7, usually at least 2–4	**Male given names:** Nikorn, Peerapat, Ronnachi, Somchai **Female given names:** Chiraporn, Jirarat, Pataree, Pornthip, Sunisa, Suwanee **Names containing:** chai, korn, kul, nee, pan/phan, pol/phol, porn/phorn, rat, ree, sak/suk, tak, wat, watta, wit, wong

examples of northern Indian and Indo-Chinese names

Table 8: Examples of northern Indian and Indo-Chinese names

Language	Examples in traditional format	Westernised examples
Hindi (and other languages spoken by north Indian Hindus)	Neelam Kumar Haresh Patil Meena Sharma Amit Thakur	(Hindi names are very seldom adapted for use in the West)
Punjabi (of Sikh religion)	Gurpreet Singh Gill Jasminder Kaur Mann Manjit Singh	Harpreet Gill Ravinder Sandhu Sukhveer Kaur Singh

Language	Examples in traditional format	Westernised examples
Khmer	Chea Sampheara Say Sok Kunthea Ung Bun Song	Sombat Kong Bopha Noun Sophy Prak
Thai	Pataree Bunnak Prathip Chaturapitapol Jiraporn Pitakthipanapong	Nui Peerapat Som Pornthip Ton Ronnachai

names from south India and Sri Lanka

Table 9: Names from south India and Sri Lanka

Language	Compo-nents	Syllables	Common components
Tamil	2–6 (usually 2–3)	2–7	**Names containing:** -an, athy, chand, dran, ingam, kumar, maniam, mugam, nathan, ragu, raj, ratna, -samy, sing(h)am, -swami/y **Other features:** names often begin with one or more initials, or contain 'd/o' or 's/o'

which language is this name from?

Language	Compo-nents	Syllables	Common components
Sinhalese	2–6 (usually 2–3)	2–7 (the surname tends to be longest)	**Names containing:** abey, -ake, ane, antha, -eke, -ge, jaya, -ke, -lage, rama, samara, sekera, sena, singhe, weera, wick **Surnames from Portuguese:** Almeida, Da Silva, Fernando, Perera

examples of names south India and Sri Lanka

Table 10: Examples of names from south India and Sri Lanka

Language	Examples in traditional format	Westernised examples
Tamil	K.S. Ravishanka Balasubramaniam s/o Selavatnarajah Ananthi Sivakumar	Gowri Janahan Kandasamy Ramanathan Bala Sathyanarayan
Sinhalese	Lasantha Pium Jayawardena Widanelage Sitha Perera Amali Ratnayake	(Sinhalese names seldom need to be Westernised)

names from Islamic Asia

The names of Asian Muslims tend to combine elements from Arabic with elements of languages spoken locally. Names such as 'Fatima' (one of the daughters of the Prophet) may be found in any Muslim community. Note the different regional spellings of the name Muhammad.

Table 11: Identifying Islamic Asian names

Language	Compo-nents	Syllables	Common components
Urdu (as used in Pakistan)	2–3	1–4 per compo-nent	**Family names:** Baig, Jatoi, Khan, Mengal, Mirza, Qureshi **Other names:** Aisha, Ali, Farah, Fatima, Fawad, Khadeeja, Muhammad, Nadeem, Sameena, Tahir, Usman, Yasir
Bangla (also called Bengali)	2–3	1–4	**Family names:** Chowdhury, Ferdeoz, Kazi, Khan, Malik, Miah, Mollah **Other names:** Men's names ending in –ur or beginning with Abdul, Bashar, Jannat, Mosammat, Mumtaz

which language is this name from?

Language	Components	Syllables	Common components
Malay	2–6	Usually about 2–4	**Male names:** Abdul, Abdullah, Ali, Azam, Faisal, Hafifi, Jamil, Mohamad, Omar, Rizwan, Sharif **Female names:** Aishah, Aminah, Azizah, Fatimah, Kamariah, Noraini, Nurul-Huda, Sharifah, Siti, Zalehra **Titles, etc.:** bin/binti, Dato (Sri)/Datuk (Sri), Hajah/Haji, Said/Syed, Sheikh, Tan/Puan Sri, Tengku/Tunku, Tun/Toh Puan
Indonesian (Javanese names)	1–4	1–6 (usually 2–3)	**Names containing:** adi, ang, -anto, -arto, budi, -ono, pras, soe, tj, -wah, -wan, -wati **Adapted English names:** Ami, Nadia, Natasha, Sonny, Tedy/Deddy, Yolanda

examples of Islamic Asian names

Table 12: Examples of Islamic Asian names

Language	Examples in traditional format	Westernised examples
Urdu (Pakistan)	Khudaija Mustafa Mengal Muhammad Tahir Mirza Ali Tahir Qureshi	(Pakistanis very seldom westernise their names)
Bangla	Firoza Akhter Mosammat Rehana Chowdhury Abidur Rahman Khan	(Bangladeshis very seldom westernise their names)
Malay	Mohd. Rashdan bin Mohd. Faisal Siti Aisha bt. Dato Jamil Nurul-Huda binti Haji Md. Rizwan	Razak Amin Mohamad Azman Hafifi Noraini Ibrahim
Indonesian	Deddy Hartono Haryanto Natasha Setiawan	Didik Didik (doubling up a single name)

Japanese names

Japanese names place the family name first, and almost always have two components of medium length. Consonants and vowels usually alternate in Japanese names.

Table 13: Identifying Japanese names

Language	Components	Syllables	Common components
Japanese	2	1–6 (usually 2–4)	**Family names:** Ito, Kobayashi, Nakamura, Saito, Sato, Suzuki, Takahashi, Tanaka, Watanabe, Yamamoto **Given names containing:** aki, chi, eri, hiro, hito, ka, kazu, ken, -ki -ko, -mi, nao, -shi, ya, yo

examples of Japanese names

Table 14: Examples of Japanese names

Language	Examples in traditional format	Westernised examples
Japanese	Ando Hideki Tanaka Makoto Watanabe Satomi	Ken Matsumoto Akiko Shinzata Sakura Yamaguchi

acknowledgements

When I began researching this book, I found surprisingly little reliable, up-to-date material on Asian names. I decided the best way to gather detailed information on naming customs was assembling all the information I could find in print and online and then cross-checking it through in-depth interviews with educated native speakers of each language. At least three people were consulted for every chapter in part two of this book, and their contributions are the foundation on which this book has been written.

I would like to express my greatest appreciation to all of the interviewees who volunteered their time and knowledge for this project. This book would not have been possible without their contributions. Some of my interviewees preferred not to be acknowledged by name, but those who were happy to be mentioned are listed below.

Shahid Akhund, Ang Tee Wee, Ernest Antoine, Leel Batugedara, Budiharto, Dr Michele Campbell, William Chao, Neelima Choahan, Choi Sunhee, Caciano & Michelle Chow, Ranjanie Ekanayake, Sien Hay, Ho Anh Gia Lê, Ihashi Mio, Ikeda Yuko, Tia Jamil, Dr Muhammad Kamal, Seenier Kandasamy, Angshuman Kar, Karamjeet Kaur, Abidur Rahman Khan, Tanzela Khan, Kim Myung Shik, Lee Suk Hyun, Liu Fulan, Fahmida Mamtaz, Bani Maula, Muhammad Ali Mirza, Ng Yee Fui, Dep

230

Nguyễn, Nikorn Nikornphan, Noguchi Sachiko, Lusia
Nurani, Phạm Liên Hương, Shiranthi Ponniah, Fathor
Rasyid, Yvonne Ratcliffe, Fawad Saeed, Karuna Sareen,
Say Sok Chinda, Kiran Sharma, Gurdeep Singh, Ranjith
& Kusumi Soysa, Tan Huey Yng, the Thai Language and
Cultural Centre, Jennifer Theunissen, Tran Anh, Trần
Thị Thu Vân, Thu Trần, Maewe Wilkins (Puangtong
Borkham), Professor Wu Yunji, Fatimah Zahroh, Khan
Kamruzzaman.

bibliography

Ager, S. 2004, 'Omniglot - a guide to written language'. <http://www.omniglot.com> [21 December 2004]

Asian forms of address 1983, Canberra: Australian Government Publishing Service.

Australasian Police Advisory Bureau, 2005. 'World religions: Police guide.' <http://www.apmab.gov.au/guide/religious2/> [30 August 2005]

Brady, A.J. and Bashar, S.A. 2005, 'Bangla – The official language of Bangladesh'. <http://www.betelco.com/bd/bangla/bangla.html> [13 September 2005]

California State Polytechnic University 2004, 'Asian name pronunciation guide'. <http://www.csupomona.edu/%7Epronunciation/> [19th March 2004]

Campbell, V. and Niven, C. 2001, *Sri Lanka*, 8th edition. Lonely Planet Publications, Melbourne.

Chitakasem, M. and Smyth, D. 1988, *Hippocrene Handy Dictionary: Thai*. Hippocrene Books Inc., New York.

Commonwealth of Australia 2003, *A guide to ethnic naming practices*. Centrelink, Canberra.

Cooper, R. and Cooper, N. 1990, *Culture Shock: Thailand*. Times Books International, Singapore.

Cummings, J. and Martin, S. 2001, *Thailand*, 9th edition. Lonely Planet Publications, Melbourne.

Dalby, A. 2004, *Dictionary of languages*. Bloomsbury Publishing, London.

De Ledesma, C., Lewis, M., and Savage, P. 1997, *Malaysia, Singapore and Brunei: The Rough Guide*. Rough Guides Ltd., London.

Dodd, J., and Lewis, M. 1998, *Vietnam: The Rough Guide*. Penguin Books Ltd., London.

Edwards, V. 2005, *Multilingual nation*. Chapters on Bengali, Chinese, Panjabi, Tamil, Urdu/Hindi, on the BBC website <http://www.bbc.co.uk/voices/multilingual/> [13 September 2005]

Ellis, C. 1996, *Culture Shock: Vietnam*. Times Books International, Singapore.

Fallon, S. 2002, *Hong Kong and Macau*. Lonely Planet Publications, Melbourne.

Florence, M. and Storey, R. 2001, *Vietnam*. Lonely Planet Publications, Melbourne.

Gordon, Ramond G., Jr. (ed.), 2005. *Ethnologue: Languages of the World*, 15th edition. SIL International, Dallas, TX. Online version: <http://www.ethnologue.com/>

Honan, M. 2001, *North India*. Lonely Planet Publications, Melbourne.

Hoang, T., Trinh, Q-T, and Nguyen, X.T. 2000, *Vietnamese Phrasebook*, 3rd edition. Lonely Planet Publications, Melbourne.

Huang, P.P.-F. 1970, *Cantonese dictionary*. New Haven & London: Yale University Press.

Huhti, T. and Mayhew, B. 1998, *South-West China*. Lonely Planet Publications, Melbourne.

IBM United States. 2004, 'Word formation in Indic languages'. <http://www-306.ibm.com/software/globalization/topics/indic/word.jsp> [20 December 2004]

International Social Service 1983, *International naming & addressing directory: A directory of naming procedures, forms of address and presentation of dates in seventy-five countries*. International Social Service in conjunction with International Social Service Australia Branch, Geneva.

Japan Reference. 2005, 'Japanese family names'. <http://www.jref.com/language/japanese_surnames.shtml> [14 November 2005]

Jones, R. 1997, *Chinese names: The traditions surrounding the use of Chinese surnames and personal names*. Pelanduk Publications, Petaling Jaya.

Khmer Institute, The. 2005, 'Common Khmer names'. <http://www.khmerinstitute.org/culture/namelist.html> [12 October 2004]

Korean Overseas Information Service. 2006, Romanization of

Korean. <http://www.korea.net/korea/kor_loca.asp?code=A020 303> [5 January 2006]

Lafayette, L. 2001, Nominecon: Developing the national ethnic names database for Electrac. Unpublished software package.

Lin, S. 1999, *What's in a Chinese name?* Federal Publications, Singapore.

Munan, H. 1997, *Culture Shock: Malaysia.* Times Books International, Singapore.

Niven, C. 1999, *Sri Lanka.* Lonely Planet Publications, Melbourne.

Plunkett, R. 2001, *South India.* Lonely Planet Publications, Melbourne.

Pragnaratne, S. 2002, *Sinhala phrasebook*, 2nd edition. Lonely Planet Publications, Melbourne.

Royal Canadian Mounted Police. 'Cross-cultural communication series: The Vietnamese'. Section of Vietnamese names. <http://www.rcmp-learning.org/vietnam/module_c.htm#CUL> [13 October 2004]

Shanson, T.L. 1997, *International guide to forms of address.* Macmillan, London.

Singapore Department of Statistics. 2004, 'Popular Chinese names in Singapore'. <http://www.singstat.gov.sg/papers/snippets/surnames. html> 20 September 2004]

Storey, R. and Park, E.K. 2001, *Korea.* Lonely Planet Publications, Melbourne.

Storey, R. 2001, *Taiwan.* Lonely Planet Publications, Melbourne.

Swan, M. and Smith, B. 2001, *Learner English : a teacher's guide to interference and other problems.* Cambridge University Press, New York.

The National Conference for Community and Justice 1989, *Asian Pacific American Handbook.* NCCJ, Los Angeles. Online version: <http://www.library.ca.gov/assets/acrobat/names.pdf>

Wilson, G. 'Devanagari lessons'. <http://www.garretwilson.com/ education/languages/hindi/devanagari/> [5 July 2004]

Zhou, C. 1991, *Minnanhua yu putonghua.* Yuwen chubanshe, Beijing.

index